Moving Forward
With Your Best Days

Moving Forward With Your Best Days

Bonnie Haak

PALMETTO
PUBLISHING
Charleston, SC
www.PalmettoPublishing.com

ISBN:9798822960107

All scripture is taken from the Holy Bible, New King James Version.

Disclosure: The first names with contributions of best days are coincidental unless personally interviewed by the author.

The author held interviews with family, friends, and individuals in the public asking this question: "What was your first best day?" In the process, she gained more friends along the way!

In loving memory of my mom,
a mother of many, an encourager, Grandma Pat,
a.k.a. Ma Beavers

CONTENTS

This book contains stand-alone chapters, which can be specifically selected by the reader in the order of their personal interest.

Part Three: Encouraging Words   137

Introduction

Have you ever been inside encouragement, where you have been given love and acceptance, forgiveness, a chance, a hug, a word, a prayer that has stuck with you?

Encouragement holds power for impacting decisions, brings healing, breaks down walls—it bears an extensive list for sure.

Are you an encourager or encouraged by someone—or both? As you read my story and others' accounts of their best days, consider how the nature of encouragement brings hope, love, and power into your life!

The search within your memory for your first best day opens up memories of other best days, bringing with it a fresh awareness to impact you and your loved ones with hope, love, and encouragement in moving forward!

Most recently I was having a conversation with my brother in Christ, Jay, Meadow's husband, in which I exclaimed, "I am so excited about this book! You know, Jay, God has healed me from an illness of more than thirty years!" Jay smiled and said, "Well,

He has done His part; now He says it is time for you to do your part and write the book!"

I inherited a love of people from my mom; because of that, I am rich in conversations and observations. As I have spent time throughout the years with people of different ages and cultures, one prominent observation has stood out to me: the human heart.

One place in my life of consistent encouragement has been to publish a book. In grade school and high school, I received awards for essay contests, poems, and spelling bees, showing promise of a gift for writing.

Now, decades later, I live on the corner of peace and quiet in a small city in Arizona, a great environment to write. However, the root cause for publishing this book comes through the power of encouragement by others.

You have potentially become part of my story—in ways we might not know about yet! The question *to capture* now is: "What was the first best day of your life?"

For certain, if you are reading this today, there is a "same" we all have in common without exception!

***

What would you do if you knew you only had twenty-four hours left?

Today, you have a presence, and today is a present!

When do you know when? When it cannot wait!

Recalling the first *best day* of your life (the very first memory that comes to your mind of all your best days) could be the key to unlocking your *best day* today to build on as you *move forward*!

In life,— we all will inevitably suffer through times of pain and sorrow. Without question, the author and her family have experienced loss, grief, health challenges, tragedies, and times of trial and error.

The author has elected to write with the main focus on the best days. The rearview mirror in a vehicle is much smaller than the windshield. Looking in the rearview mirror has its place, as does keeping eyes on the windshield for moving forward.

The thought to consider here is when people are stretched, even to the point of hanging on by a thread, can be a time when character becomes sharpened: compassion can be extended, strength grows in the face of adversity, perseverance is developed to go the distance, and discernment develops to know how and when to choose. It is often in the valleys where empathy is born, hope is sought, and faith is strengthened.

Part One

Best Days

Chapter 1

Families

Traditions. Triumphs. Permissions.

Some of my best days, growing up in my big family:

When I was seven, I realized how fun and funny my mom was, which resulted in a lack of frown lines on her lovely face. She was young at heart because she could see "with the eyes of a child." She was young in years as well and grew up with her children.

My oldest brother, Jimmy, would answer the door, and his friend would ask, "Can your mom play?" True story. Jimmy was six years old, and mom was twenty.

Growing up in Arizona in the '60s and '70s, I was the middle of eight children; it was an adventure and challenging too.

Mom would give each of her children a five-dollar bill to buy family presents at Christmastime. We learned how to stretch a five-dollar bill, probably because penny candy was still available back then! In the process, she was instilling the realization that the amount spent on the gift was not as important as the joy in giving it, however small it might be. This was the beginning of my belief that simple is best.

Mom would sit down with all of us to show us how to make paper chains, popcorn strings, and homemade ornaments. Afterward, we would trim our Christmas tree, with each one of us hanging their ornaments on the tree, giving loving permission for the glee of a child, along with a real sense of ownership.

1969 Christmas tree Polaroid picture
Mom, thirty-one years old

Mom was carefree; she used to dance with the broom to country and western music in between her daily chores, played jacks and building blocks with her children, loved to tell jokes, participated in family card games, laughed from the belly and sometimes snorted while laughing and holding her hand over her mouth, loved to dip her fishing pole in the water, and loved her family and her neighbors.

Mom and her funny laugh (pun intended)

Mom's favorite fishing spot, Cave Lake
When she lived in Ely, Nevada, anyway!

Mom did not know a stranger and would give away her last dollar if someone needed one. She never possessed money beyond what covered the basics (eight kids) but was rich in love and relationships. My brother Bert likes to say what Mom could do with hydrogen peroxide, baking soda, and Mentholatum, Dad could do with duct tape, baling wire, and J-B Weld. Mom was not one to panic; when her kids were sick, she would inevitably nurse them back to health. I used to think Mentholatum's main ingredient was love when my mom would doctor me with it.

When I was eleven years old, I noticed one day my mom was super sad. I had not seen her this way before and asked her why she was upset. She told me that it was Cindy's birthday.

Cindy was mom's little three-year-old daughter. In 1957, Mom was nineteen years old and at home with her two children. The butane tank had run out of gas; the man came to fill the tank and did not check inside for proper safety. The living room heater blew, blowing out the windows and flames engulfed the room. Mom and Jimmy were in the kitchen; Mom ran into the living room through the flames to get Cindy. She handed Jimmy out the living room window and carried Cindy out in her arms. A church member came and drove them to the hospital. Grandma Grace Whipple traveled with them, holding Cindy in her arms. Cindy kept asking her grandma, "Why are you crying?" She passed away at the hospital in her grandma's arms. Jimmy, age five, was burned on his arms and hands. Mom was burned on her face, back, arms, hands, and legs. Mom spent three weeks in a burn unit to debride her burns. My aunt Patsy took care of Jimmy once he was discharged from the hospital.

As hard as it was for me to hear this and to see my mom cry, I felt closer to her than ever and gained a full-on appreciation for her loving and relaxed way. At age eleven, I became close to my mom in a most special way.

Mom knew how to stretch a dollar, buying potatoes by the 100-pound sack sometimes; pinto beans and flour in bulk. She knew the art of bartering. I joked with her that she would drive a hundred miles to save fifty cents.

Mom made the best homemade bread and dinner rolls and sometimes fry bread when there was enough bread dough. She always offered hot buttered bread slices to our friends who came in the door with us. Bread right out of the oven is a generous gift, as the loaf only goes half as far. She made Redeye gravy when we were fortunate enough to have breakfast ham with grits and eggs. Another food Mom cooked, from the South, was fatback, sometimes called "poor man's bacon." We loved fatback and considered that we were living high on the hog (pun on purpose) when we had it to eat. Our granny who lived in South Carolina would pack the fatback in a bed of thick newspapers and mail it to us; our anticipation would build for its arrival.

Granny also sent big boxes of hand-me-downs on occasion (in our family there was no such thing as gently used; we were a rough bunch)! When those boxes arrived, we were so excited to go through our cousins' clothes and have new ones to wear to school.

My granny was a remarkable woman, a force to be reckoned with. Because we lived in Arizona, and she lived in South Carolina, we did not see her or Granddaddy often while we were growing up.

When Granny came to our house in Arizona, we knew we would have to toe the line! She meant what she said and said what she meant. At lunchtime, Granny would open the door of the house and yell, "You children better get in here now or I'm going to whoop y'all!" We would run like ants to the sugar hill. Although she was stern, Granny was a marshmallow on the inside, and had one of the kindest hearts of anyone I ever knew. She had a special gift; she could take a crying baby, place it onto her large soft shoulder, whereas the baby could not be consoled before it would immediately stop crying! Granddaddy was a hard worker; he was kind and a man of faith in God. In their family of ten children, they had three sons who were born with Duchenne's muscular dystrophy, requiring three wheelchairs.

Grandaddy was Baptist, a PK; Granny was Pentecostal. I guess that makes me a Bapti-Costal. Actually, the Lord called me into interdenominational ministry at some point in my Christian walk.

Grandma Beavers was our grandma who lived across the street in Arizona. She was another one who was young at heart, loving, and truly kind! She was there for us because she was retired, and she was all about family. Grandma taught me the process of making grape jelly, as she had grapevines in her yard. She would turn her TV on for my special TV show series, and she patiently tried teaching me about quilting.

One time my Grandma Beavers and I got a novel idea to put on fake fingernails. We sat in her living room, applying the fake nails, and decided if we pushed them up under the cuticle a little, they would look more real. The next day we realized that we had made a big mistake, as our cuticles were protesting the invasion. We went to the local store and thankfully they had the right product to remove our fake nails, which removed the pain. There was only a little lingering embarrassment left.

***

When I was nineteen, I was riding our mare, Babe, when she bucked me off. This was a surprise, but I found out later when the accompanying horse and rider went to the barn that Babe, as the boss mare, decided to buck me off and head for the barn. I hope this explains why, at the time when I had a full arm cast, I did not consider riding Babe to be a risk.

I was in a fetal position on the ground.

Dad, who was watching out the window, came to help. He said, "Are you OK, Sis?"

I responded, "Dad, I think I broke my back."

He told me to stand up slowly and cross my arms in front of my chest. Standing at six feet six, he easily wrapped his arms around my upper body and gently but firmly shook me a couple of times. Directly after, I heard my back pop, and the pain left!

My dad walked me back to the ranch house. He ran a bath with warm water and added Epsom salts.

He handed me an ice pack for my swollen thumb where the edge of the cast threatened to cut off my circulation. He told me to soak in the bathtub with the ice pack on the swelling. Some people would call this a rancher's remedy; for me, "That's my dad!"

Howard E. Whipple

Bob, Bonnie, Grandpa,
Ben and David

The first night I danced with Bob, my future husband, little did I know we would be married for thirty-nine years, parent four sons, and experience the joy of grandparenting! Bob was tall and handsome, a little shy, yet he showed solid confidence.

A week later, we went on a date to Bodie, an old ghost town in California, taking my three-year-old son with us. As we traveled back, we were in the cab of Bob's truck, and Ben was fast asleep with one foot resting on Bob's leg. Bob was rubbing his foot while we enjoyed easy conversation, and I thought to myself, "I could truly like this man."

Bob and I felt a sense of vulnerability, a hesitancy to get too close to each other, because we both had been married previously.

Our next date was going to the circus with our boys in tow. From the circus date we graduated to a scuba diving date, where we went diving in northern California at Fort Bragg. Abalone diving, a free-water dive (no tanks), proved to be challenging and fun.

However, when we went scuba diving the next day, we were forty feet down, when I became entangled in some kelp, which was pulling on my mask! My first priority in this dilemma was to keep the regulator in my mouth! As certified PADI scuba divers, we had been trained to always use the "buddy system" and have the smaller person in front, to stay calm in difficult situations so as not to deplete your air supply too quickly. Well, I remembered both these instructions, but Bob was nowhere in sight!

I did manage to stay calm and untangle myself from the kelp. I swam to the surface, and there was Bob, which was another important part of our training certification. If you lose each other—surface—it is nearly impossible to find each other in a deep expanse of a body of water.

Bob felt he could talk with me about anything, something he had not found in his life before us. He often told me that I was really easy to talk with.

Bob was a Harley man, and I was a horse-woman. I would ride on the back of his motorcycle from time to time, but he let me know quickly in our relationship that he would never ride a horse with me because they do not have a "kill switch!"

***

The first day of meeting Bob's family was interesting and exciting too. I was nervous. It was Christmastime. Esther, my future mother-in-law, handed me a present, and my heart melted. A real icebreaker. Not the gift, but the thought.

Esther was an amazing cook. One of our sons commented that she set the table with style, and she did! She was a sensitive lady with a kind heart. She believed a baby is God's greatest work of art. She was an encouragement in my faith, as she gave me my first Bible. My future father-in-law, Ben, was a family man. He loved working in his woodshop, golfing, and being present in the home in his retirement years.

***

After dating for a year, Bob and I got married. We had a blended family. My husband had two sons from his previous marriage, I had one son from my previous marriage, and two years later, we had a son. The love in our family was undeniable. Despite the special challenges we faced as a blended family, our close ties were noticed by others. People in our small town and even our neighbors had a hard time figuring out who belonged to whom. We would chuckle and say, "They are all ours."

***

Every year, when deer season was open, Bob would go hunting and almost always came back with a deer. The few times he came home without one, his building partner and close friend, Troy Madraso, would generously give our family deer meat from his freezer. I never did hunt—I just couldn't—but I was happy to sit with my husband at the table in our home for two to three days to butcher the deer meat. We quickly discovered that ground venison makes the best tacos you will ever eat—at least our family thought so and others we invited over. We usually did not disclose the venison part.

Ceviche was a favorite dish in our family. We learned this from our Christian friends Mark and Graciela, as they blessed us and gave us the recipe as well. Their ceviche recipe consisted of imitation crab legs, cooked shrimp (no tails), baby clams, Clamato juice, celery, cucumber (diced and peeled, center removed).

One day, my husband took a big bowl of the ceviche to share with coworkers. A coworker asked what was in the ceviche, as she watched others readily spooning it into their bowls. As she was hesitant about enjoying this expensive and rare blessing, my husband, who was dipping the ladle to get his portion, pointed to the baby clams and said, "These are sea urchin testicles." She wrinkled her nose and then took a pass.

***

We were on a day trip to the mountains to cut down our Christmas tree. Snow was in abundance everywhere we went. We found a spot with pinyon pine trees. We parked, and my husband got out to scout the area for our Christmas tree. I was sitting in the cab of the truck with Ben, who was four years old. Bob was coming back toward the truck; we rolled the cab window down, hollering at Bob and laughing. Bob made a snowball and lobbed it toward the cab of the truck. Ben was laughing, and that snowball landed right in his mouth! He was struggling to breathe, and I was laughing so hard I could barely help him.

We cut our tree down, loaded it in the truck, and headed for home. I made some hot chocolate, and we sat down at the table to make paper chains and popcorn strings as decorations. Thank you, Mom, Grandma Pat.

***

In our small town, there was a Young Citizens Activity Center a few blocks from our home. The program director was an outstanding individual with a passion for young people to have opportunities in community sports. This was a saving grace for our family, as all our sons were athletic.

We followed the athletics trail where our four sons were involved. We had purchased a Suburban, and it became a second home as we traveled around the state of Nevada for high school sports. It was an amazing time for all of us!

Ben showing off his serious "hops"

We went on a camping trip, all six of us, in our Suburban to northern Nevada. We explored the Lehman Caves, where there were stalactites and stalagmites everywhere. Beautiful! It was a little tricky for us because we have a tall family. We had almost made it out of the cave when Bob didn't quite make the duck under a low-hanging stalactite. Ouch!

Next, we traveled on over to Cave Lake; it was breathtaking, with the greenest water I had ever seen.

The first night we were there, one of our sons told us about crawdad capturing and showed us the art of it. We used bacon for bait, and Bob held a light toward the water so the boys could spot the crawdads feeding. They would wade into the water and grab the crawdad by its' back, carefully watching the pincers that threatened to connect with their fingers and then throw them into a bucket of water. We fished for crawdads until midnight!

I was as excited as, or more excited than they were, but I did not participate in getting the crawdads. I knew I would be the cook—or that was my personal excuse because I did not want to connect with crawdad pincers.

We saw people fishing off the dock the next day for crawdads. They would tie a chicken leg onto a long string and lower it into the water; when they brought the string back up, with crawdads feeding on the chicken leg, I was fascinated and impressed.

Later, when we got back home from our camping trip, I called my brother and asked him how to cook the crawdads. We had crawdads in our kitchen sink that had been on ice for the trip back. We opened the salt container and shook salt over the crawdads. There is an important reason to take this step: it makes them poop. If you have ever deveined shrimp, you can appreciate how easy this method actually is!

Here is the recipe: Corn on the cob, halved; red potatoes; mushrooms; onions; Zatarain's seasoning; crawdads. In a large pot filled two-thirds with water, set the heat to high. Once the water is boiling, add in all the ingredients, except the crawdads. When the soup returns to a boil, turn the heat to medium-low until the vegetables are tender. Add in the crawdads, and bring to a rolling boil for three minutes. Serve with bread and dessert.

***

Our home was filled with pranks, an abundance of home-cooked meals, and an interesting variety of critters. When our television needed repair, we asked our sons, "Do you want a new TV or a dishwasher?" They voted unanimously for the dishwasher as we had never owned one, and they each took their turn to wash the dishes. Three years later, we purchased our new television.

We protected our family dinner hour. No answering the phone, no television. This opened up opportunities for good conversations. One thing though: Our family members would show a serious methodical nodding of the head, while slowly chewing their food, indicating the meal was outstanding. Words were not needed; that would interrupt the savoring of the flavoring!

Because I grew up in a large family and did not have many choices in the basics, which had served me well, as a mom, I chose not to run a cafeteria for my crew. We ate the same foods; when food was left on the plate, it was placed in the kitchen, no evening snacks or dessert until their dinner was finished. Rarely did any food go into the garbage can. Today, they are healthy and tall men. We can thank Grandma Pat for the food part and Grandpa Whipple for the genes.

***

The first day Ben's wife gave birth to their son, our grandson, I found myself overcome with elation for them, for him, for us! We cherished being there as our son held his little boy with such tenderness and wonderment. Ben's wife was so peaceful, happy, and content as she held their amazing little baby boy in her arms. Their family was complete when, three years later, they had their precious baby girl.

***

We were blessed with yet another grandson and daughter-in-law in our family when our youngest son David married!

Like father, like son

*Our gentle Maine Coon (Hector),
who we trapped in the wild as a kitty*

***

It was a fun day when my husband and I brought our puppy Laverne home when she was seven weeks old. Our oldest grandson would lie down on the carpet, and Laverne would run back and forth across his back and bite his hair. Our grandson tried to dodge all the puppy-tickle-licks by turning his head from side to side while his giggles filled the room and our hearts. I brought Shirley home this year, who is cute as a bug's ear. Laverne is brown and white; Shirley is jet black and white. Laverne is taller than Shirley. Hmm, not exactly planned that way, but we burst out laughing when we realized it!

Evelyn: Her best day ever was one spring afternoon when her dad picked her up from school. She was turning nine years old and remembers the day was very beautiful in April. The flowers were blooming, and green was everywhere. She noticed a big bag in the car with clothes in it. Her dad said, "It's for you!" Filled with excitement, she opened the bag, and inside were three beautiful dresses! Her dad asked her what she wanted to do for her birthday. All she could think about was ice cream and the park since it was so nice outside. She remembers enjoying the ice cream and a cool spring breeze on her face while being with her dad. The one-on-one time she had with him was special to her, more than anything else!

Chapter 2

Roads

Adventurous. Narrow. Forgiveness.
Dedicated to My Mom, the Road Warrior

The day when we moved from Globe, Arizona, to Roosevelt Estates (close to Roosevelt Lake, Arizona) was the start of a crazy-fun adventure for myself and my siblings. I was nine years old.

On Christmas morning, we were in the living room opening presents when my mom said to open the front door.

Outside there were seven bicycles lined up, side-by-side. We went wild! Those bicycles were our best route to fun and mischief as we rode them on the dirt road around our block. We soon graduated to riding our bikes to the swimming hole, where we would spend half a day swimming, then return home for Mom's hearty home-cooked meal.

Mom was the greatest cook, southern style! Her food had love inside it; you could taste it actually, because of the joy she served it up with. She became well known for her homemade bread, always offering slices of hot bread to our friends who came inside with us. She was well known for her homemade tamales, making 200-300 at a time. Mom involved her kids in the tamale-making process: cleaning the husks, stirring the masa, and rolling the tamales. Then there was taste testing to see if anything needed to be changed; this was our favorite part of helping.

When Mom went fishing, she would take anyone who wanted to go. We would travel a short distance to Roosevelt Lake for a few hours of catfishing. Once back home, that evening, we would eat fried catfish dipped in flour and cornmeal for dinner.

Great-Grandpa Rae was known for his pecan pies. An absolute requirement was that the fresh pecans had to come from Texas. Our family would sit at the dining room table, shelling a mound of pecans and having some lively conversation. Grandpa took great joy in making six or more pecan pies during the holidays.

My mom and aunts would beg Grandpa for the recipe, but he would not budge on giving it out; the recipe was inherited when he passed away at eighty-three years old.

Every single time, this family activity would take me back to the memories of stringing popcorn and making paper chains every year for the Christmas tree with my family.

***

My older brother Mike Whipple introduced us to cow-pie flipping with a stick. Most of the time underneath the cow pie, we would find a scorpion; using our stick, we would herd the scorpion into a glass jar. Then we would take them home to our mom. The funny thing is I do not remember what happened to our "pet scorpions" beyond that point! Not too much fazed my mom; as a mother of nine, she had seen it all!

When it rained hard, frogs were flooded out of

their burrows. My siblings and I would stack three tires and fill the inside of each tire with some water. We would go frog hunting, sometimes reaching into a burrow and pulling a frog out. We would rescue them off the roads to save them from their demise of the "other tires."

We would then place them inside their new home. The tires were high enough and the circumference was small enough so they could not jump out, yet they had a swimming pool inside the tires. We loved our frog farms and at one point had 200 frogs in two farms. After a few days, we would release the colonies of frogs to go back to their environments.

We went on hikes to the "cracks," mountains where the face had been carved out by the rains. Each one of us took a scrap of cardboard to sit on and use as a "slide" down the mountain.

Our favorite outside family fun was Roll-A-Bat. We had enough people in our family to play ball; sometimes we would call Uncle Larry, Aunt Lola, and our cousins. Whoever was available would hurry over to join in on the fun!

Once we were gathered together, we would designate a pitcher and a batter; everyone else was out in the field. The pitcher would pitch the ball. If the batter hit the ball, whoever retrieved it in the field would roll the ball on the ground to try to hit the bat, which was positioned on the ground facing the direction of the outfielder. If the ball hit the bat—which was always interesting to watch because the ground could hold surprises like dirt clods, rocks, and valleys—then the outfielder would switch places with the batter.

***

The first day my husband and I moved from Nevada to Arizona to retire was surreal. We opted to lease a house so we could dwell in the Casa Grande area to see if we liked it. We loved it! A few months later, we purchased a home. We had five points for our move, primarily for health reasons:

- Closer medical facilities
- Affordable homes
- Family relatively close (pun on purpose)
- Hot weather
- Interdenominational ministry

Bob and I had never been to Casa Grande, Arizona, before. Prior to our move, Bob's old high school friend Chuck stopped by our house there in Nevada on his way to Hot August Nights in Reno, Nevada. As Chuck sat at our kitchen table, he mentioned that he lived in Casa Grande, which we had no knowledge of because Bob had not seen him for fifty years.

Well...I had been looking at homes in Casa Grande on the internet. Really, it was like God cupped His hands and yelled down from heaven, "It is OK for you to go now, Bob and Bonnie!" We were in awe—no coincidence there.

We retired in Arizona, but not really, as we were serving in varying capacities in our new community. Our favorite phrase as retirees quickly became "we have options" —what time to get up in the morning, whether or not to attend fundraisers, when to go to the grocery store, and how to better keep our cool in the driver's seat during busy and sometimes crazy traffic—and of course, staying in a peaceful state in checkout lines in the store.

Not having work schedules was a wonderful place to be in life. Ahh...we remained incredibly thankful to have our health and each other to be able to enjoy some retirement time in our lives.

Chapter 3

Miracles

Life. Hope. Faith.

I was twenty years old the first day I gazed into the face of my firstborn, and my heart began to swell as if it were leaving my chest. He was the most incredible baby; he was strong, lifting his head off my shoulder immediately. His physical strength and a strong character stayed with him as he grew. I wrapped him in my arms, breathing in his goodness, and then I felt the intense emotion of being a proud mom, thankful for the blessing of my son Ben. What a miracle—one of the best miracles on this side of heaven!

Grandma Pat loving on Ben

When our youngest son was born, we felt such amazement and thankfulness! I had teased Bob about having one more baby after this one, and we would have a basketball team if we had another boy. We agreed that our family was complete with our four sons.

This son was a big boy, tall; he almost stepped out of the womb. Although he started with a healthy birth weight, it was his vertical growth rate that was sometimes a little startling.

When David was two months old, my good friend Doris Inman came over with a gift and to see him. We were sitting in the living room, and she said to me, "Bonnie, are you going to get your baby?"

"He is right there in the baby swing."

"Oh, he is so big. I thought you were babysitting!"

David with his Grandma Pat

I worked for a nonprofit company that was in an area where there were three-story apartments across the street. I was leaving my office and trying to secure the door from the outside. The dead bolt had not been working well for a few weeks. I was feeling some frustration as I had been trying to lock the door for several minutes; suddenly, the dead bolt made the sound of locking. I looked, and sure enough it was locked, but I did not lock it—as I was not involved with an attempt at that time.

I walked over to my vehicle and got inside. Then, I noticed there was a younger man looking at me through the window. I did not feel fear and did not hit the lock button, as I knew he could break the glass... or worse. As I prepared to back out, I saw there were two more men behind my car. I inched back slowly, and then I noticed a truck coming down the street, which stopped to wait for me. I backed on out and then proceeded up the street.

As I traveled and pondered everything that had taken place, there was absolutely no question in my mind as to who threw that dead bolt across and why.

Something I have learned in my life is that when people can first see the little miracles, this is where our faith will grow with the greater miracles.

Brian: He said his best day was when he was a kid, riding his bicycle, swinging across a pond on a rope with a tire tied to a tree, and taking a plunge into the water. He said he lived in Philadelphia really close to the Philadelphia Folk Festival in the '70s. As we talked, I noticed that he had laugh lines around his eyes and a friendly face. Brian was in a vehicle accident in 1991 and lost both legs above his knees; it was evident to me that he was choosing to keep *moving forward.*

Antonio: His best day was when his team won a flag football championship in the third grade. His grandma was the only person in his family to attend the game; it is a special memory for him, as she has since passed away.

Olga: She found out she was pregnant on Christmas Eve with her first son. Her best first day was when he was born on August 29, 2003.

Two years later, on Christmas Eve, by God's providential hand, she received a call from an adoption agency asking if they wanted to adopt their second son. The adoption became final ten months later! Christmas Eve is another best day, threefold, for Olga and her family!

***

I will always remember the first day I heard this story about a little preborn baby in heaven asking Jesus about her mother, a story to share:

The baby asks Jesus, "Does my mother love me?"
Jesus answers, "Yes, she loves you very much."
"When will she be here?"
"It will not be too long."
"Are you sure she will be here?"
"I'm sure, because she asked me to forgive her."
"What did she do?"
"I don't remember."
The Baby then goes back to sleep.

I am thankful for this story; it lines up with God's truth.

Forgiveness comes with asking, believing, and receiving.

Chapter 4

Coming through the Valleys

Perseverance. Faith. Grace.

The day I learned more about crying through the throat, I was in the hospital room with my son and daughter-in-law who was recovering from back surgery. When we entered the room, I hugged my son who does not often show his emotions. As we hugged, I could feel his throat moving as he swallowed his tears, which were wanting to emerge. The imperceptible can speak volumes, and my heart became even softer for them.

***

The first day when I realized my mom had come back into her faith, I had noticed a difference in her. I asked my sisters if they saw it, too, and they had.

Mom grew up in a Christian home; married at age thirteen, which was common in the South back then. She had led an interesting life. She kept her faith but did not walk in it; yet if you knew her well, she would testify in ways that showed her belief in God. For one thing, if we said, "holy cow," she would reprimand us that "holy" is only for "Holy." Many times, she stated that she believed in miracles, which was a seed for my faith.

At age sixty-eight, my mom ran back into the open arms of Jesus! He had been with her all her life, faithfully and lovingly waiting for her to come back to Him. She finished her Race at age seventy-three.

Audrey: Her first best day was when she became a mother. She was in labor for three days and was not dilating fast enough. She would go to the hospital, and they would advise her to return home until she dilated more.

Her labor progressed, and she was finally admitted to the hospital. By that time, due to lack of rest and increasing anxiety, the pain became so bad that she agreed to an epidural, but eventually was given Pitocin, and that made everything worse because she could feel the pain despite the epidural.

She was not progressing and was screaming in pain. It just felt like forever and ever that she was in pain. Her mother-in-law was getting worried because she had been in the hospital for a day and a half. She got to the point where she was at nine centimeters, but she was stuck.

Her mother-in-law, who was a nurse by profession, said she was going to talk to the nurses. She approached the nurses' station and said, "You guys need to get the doctor down here because something is not right."

The nurse responded, "Oh, let nature take its course; everything is fine."

Her mother-in-law said, "No, something is wrong. Please get the doctor down here."

The doctor came and checked Audrey's and the baby's vitals. The baby's heart rate was dropping. Audrey was wheeled into an emergency C-section.

This whole time, Audrey was praying to God, "Please, God. I love my daughter. I have not even met her yet, but I want her to live. I want us both to live. I promise, God, if we get out of this OK, I will be a better Christian. I will have better faith because I know my faith has been slipping a little bit."

The C-section was pretty intense. They pulled the baby out, and she was blue; the cord was wrapped around her neck, and she had swallowed her meconium.

The baby ended up having to stay in the NICU for a week, but she was OK. Audrey ended up being OK too. She was recovering; getting cut open was a lot, but she did not even care. She was thankful to God. When she held her daughter for the first time, she felt so happy, the happiest she had ever felt in her entire life. Audrey's best day!

Even now when she looks at her four-year-old daughter, she remains so grateful and thankful to God to have her in her life.

Sharen: Struggling with fibromyalgia, she would sometimes feel guilty for resting. She was reminded in His word that God gives permission to rest. When she chooses to rest without guilt, the Lord comes, because that is His favorite time. He does not like to come when we are too busy or too loud, or when we are listening to other stuff. From the time He comes in a quiet moment, one can know that what He reveals *in that moment* is worth living one's life by.

Mary: She had a hard time with severe asthma. The medication she was taking put her behind in school, and she had dyslexia on top of everything else. The teachers did not know about learning disabilities back then. She was considered dumb and lazy. She had no self-esteem. When she was in high school, there was a work program in which she could go to school for half a day and work for half a day.

As a junior in high school, she was placed in the work program and hired to work in a flower shop. She so loved working there and discovered she had a gift for designing flower arrangements. Mary worked at the flower shop for several years.

She remembers that her best day was when school opened back up for the students, and she did not have to go. This was the most wonderful day because she felt free, grown up, and important as she drove to work.

Petra: When she was first diagnosed with macular degeneration, an eye disease, she was pretty angry and scared. The disease allows only peripheral vision at its advanced stages. After a couple of weeks, she accepted the diagnosis and was impressed upon by the Lord to make her life simpler in preparation of a decreasing vision. In the process of simplifying, the Lord showed her that what you have plenty of is not really giving, but to give up completely something you own is sacrificial giving, and this was what He wanted her to do. She cried sometimes as she found new homes for her books, which she had kept all her life, but she trusted in God's leading. Petra and her husband had a tender conversation in which her husband told her that he would be her eyes, and she could be his hands. These difficult places have been so much more bearable with the Lord in there, helping them.

Charlene: She said she only had to think for a moment to call to memory her first best day. When she was a young woman, she had been in bondage to a drug addiction for ten years, when she was set free by her Lord and Savior Jesus Christ!

Inside the grip of her addiction, she struggled with guilt and shame, with her head down. When she started her walk with Jesus, He took the guilt and shame from her, and gently lifted her head to look up. And she found herself in awe as she gazed at the stars in the night sky. Stars she had never seen before!

He counts the number of the stars; He calls them all by name.

– Psalm 147:4

Chapter 5

Bridges

Reconciliations. Ultimate. The Gift of Time.

My son Ben told me about an opportunity that he had to communicate with a man who was deaf and blind and said of anything he had experienced in his twenty-seven years; this was the ultimate. He was seated across from the blind and deaf man and signed into his hand to have a conversation with him.

***

Running a campaign for election to the school board was more fun than I would have anticipated. I spent a total of $129 for my campaign. I did not join in with putting up election signs in the community. Instead, I chose to make some business cards:

Elect Bonnie Haak for School Board Trustee
My Campaign for School Board Trustee over the Past Twenty Years:
Junior-High-Level Math/Science Tutor

Assisted Seniors with Scholarship Applications
Parent Representative on Attendance Advisory Board
Volunteer Playground/Classroom Monitor
Involvement in Graduation Celebrations / Class Trips
Character Traits and Abilities I Will Contribute:
Strong Accounting/Budgeting Skills
Commitment/Decisions for the Best Education

I asked some of my young friends to make campaign signs for me and gave them poster boards, crayons, and markers. As they made the signs, I educated them on what a school board member does for the schools. And we took their three campaign signs and attached them to chain-link fences at homes in the neighborhood.

Blessings are often missed in looking for perffectionism. I believe perfectionism is a trap. One place I love to be is in signing a card or a sign-up sheet even, where all signatures are in a row, to include my signature across the page with some flair. It can be a place of encouragement to others. Really, it makes me think of the elevator opening with a person facing the opposite way, when people enter and the elevator opens on the next floor, everyone is facing the opposite way! No harm-no foul type opportunities.

***

The primary election's results were the initial six candidates to two candidates moving forward for the general election.

Then there was the campaign speech:

My primary goals as a potential board member are to work toward effective solutions and to give encouragement to our children and school personnel. These are the premises of my decision in filing for school trustee.

I have served three years on the attendance advisory board for our local school district. Currently I serve on the chamber of commerce and the Family Resource Center boards, both of which I intend to discontinue at the first of the year if elected for school board.

If elected, I will work diligently and honestly to do my part as a board member to work toward the best programs and policies for our district.

My challenge to you is when you vote, consider it carefully; then step in as often as you can to attend school board meetings. Get involved at every opportunity your schedule permits, to the benefit of our future generations...as a parent, grandparent, or as a concerned citizen of our community and country.

As a mother and citizen within our community, I have a good background in our schools and also some ideas for the future of our schools. Throughout the past twenty years, I have been actively involved within our school district, supportive of the teaching staff and administration, and have assisted in different areas and programs.

I am trusting you will vote on November 2 and fully support your new board, exercising two of the many freedoms we have in the good ol' U.S. of A.

***

Once elected as a school board member, I became part of a bridge for the students, staff, and the superintendent for four schools within the school district.

The first day I served on the Mineral County School Board was amazing! I attended a school board conference prior to serving on the board, where I felt like a kid in a candy store.

At the conference, there was a "mock school board" demonstration. I could hardly wait to put one together for our school district and community, which consisted of seven students from the government class, all seniors.

Some of the students got involved in making 130 burritos and other preparations for the event. One teacher asked me, "Bonnie, how do you get these students to do all of this?"

I responded, "With encouragement and trust."

On the night of the mock school board presentation, Monday, March 21, 2005, the community attendance was remarkable. The high school students made incredible board members, teaching me a thing or two in the process. What a "prerequisite" they turned out to be!

The high school seniors and I had placed a donation jar on the counter, where we set up the food and drinks. The high school seniors agreed the money donation should go toward "the Big Flag Project" with special appreciation to our armed forces who have and continue to protect the United States of America Flag and our freedom. They said they wanted to look up at the US flag in their hometown and feel proud of their personal contribution to be a part of it.

The day I walked beside an elementary school principal, in conversation regarding classroom presentations for bullying prevention and volunteer monitors for playground supervision, I knew without question I was in the right space. It was exactly why I accepted the opportunity to chair the Bullying Prevention Committee of the school district as a board member.

The children on the playgrounds affectionally tagged us as "safety specialists" as we walked among them with our clipboards during recess.

Serving as a board member, there were many opportunities to present in the classrooms. My favorite topics of interaction with the classroom students were bringing education regarding our US soldiers serving overseas and bullying prevention in the schools. Interacting with the students was, without question, my favorite place to be!

There are four types of bullies:
- Physical
- Verbal
- Relational
- Cyberbullying

The bully has "power" over their target, by size, authority, or a group of people under the bully's control (e.g., gangs, cliques, or previous victims).

***

But there was more. The board selected me to hand out diplomas at the high school graduation. So there I was, an elected official, handing my son his high school diploma for his graduation. It does not get too much better than that!

**

We do not have to do everything, but we can do something. Love builds bridges...

The first day I learned about the "bridge illustration," I found this picture to be simple yet powerful at the same time. In this depiction, there is a deep void flanked by two mountains far apart from one another.

A person is standing at the edge of a mountain.

God in His infinite love for all of humanity stands at the edge of another mountain.

The person sees God and does not know how to get there to be with Him.

Then Jesus brings His cross and places it inside the void...

And is nailed to the Cross, dies on the Cross, for the whole world's sin.

Romans 3:23
Luke 24:7
John 6:47

It is never ever too late to cross this Bridge.
A decision. A choice.

Chapter 6

Mountain Tops

Overcomer. Elation. Strength.

Early one Sunday morning, we headed for the mountain with excitement, taking our seventeen-year-old son fishing for the day. Once there, our excitement turned into exhilaration—being out of doors together as a family, with our faith, fishing poles, and food. A place where joy abounds, conversation flows, and the food tastes great!

Lois: Her first best day was when she got married forty-five years ago to her best friend. She was excited to have someone to share life with, to do things with; not just anyone, but with her best friend!

Her eyes welled up with tears as she was telling me her first best day. When I asked if her husband had passed, she responded, "No." Her tears of happiness said it all.

Mary: The day after Mary's wedding to Brian, there was no honeymoon for them. They both had to work on Monday. They loved camping with their family and friends, and there was an RV show at the local fairgrounds on Sunday. She felt so free as they walked around looking at the RVs, wishing they could have one someday. For the first time, Mary was on her own with her new husband. She did not have to report where she was or what she was doing. This made her feel grown up. As they walked hand in hand, meeting people, she was so proud to be married. Currently, Brian and Mary have been married fifty-one years!

Eric: His best days are with his family. He said, with great excitement, that to be with his family, eating with them and joking around with them is his best place. He said once he closes the door and is inside his home, he has the freedom to do what he wants and mostly to love his family.

He emphasized that it is important to protect your family; if you lose them and later get them back, it will not be at 100 percent. He likened this to spilling a cup of water; when you pick it back up, you will have lost some of it. As husband and father, Eric said, "Above all, protect your family."

Debby: She had been on a long journey trying to conceive. At the age of twenty-nine, she had a hysterectomy due to endometriosis. That dream was gone. She decided she did not want to adopt and was not going to have children. She went through another year of feeling a gnawing emptiness. One day she realized God had given her a large capacity to love. And she gave herself permission to adopt. She understood she could love adopted babies just as if she had given birth to them.

Three more years passed, and then they finally got the opportunity to adopt two little girls, sisters, ages three and four! The next nineteen years were full of ups and downs, happy times, and sad times, as her love continued to grow stronger for her daughters.

Her youngest daughter, at the age of nineteen, was in the delivery room to deliver her first child. Debby was there, too, from the start for the birth of her first grandchild. She encouraged and loved her daughter through the intense work of delivering the baby. When her granddaughter was born, she saw her little head come out and then her eyes opened wide, which was a shock. It was then Debby knew she was at the point of her life she had been trying so hard to get to. She felt so fulfilled, so much love, so much forgiveness for the burdens she had been carrying. It was the moment Debby had been waiting for her whole life.

Terry: God was very gentle with him. His friend Wes once told Terry he had prayed for him for two years. Terry said God has a way of getting our attention.

Wes had invited him to church. Terry had been waiting to go to a party, to get polluted and all that kind of stuff. It was about 8:30 p.m., somewhere in there, and his thing was to never go to a party before 9:00 p.m. Terry was reading the Bible when he read Romans 10:9. He kept on reading, looking at the clock, and something pulled Terry back to Romans 10:9. He read it again, and he got that flash of Jesus Christ in his life; God used that verse to save him.

Terry knew about God, but he had no respect for Him, no interest in Him. But that night, and it has been so long ago, he had no interest in the party. Instead, he had a party with Jesus that night.

He has known Him and loved Him, and God has taken care of Terry ever since. All the wonderful brothers and sisters that he has met have been really encouraging to him.

Terry's salvation from that night has been assured; he knew he was saved, and he went along with it. He said we slip and slide and fall, but he always knew his salvation. Terry felt bad one time because he had slipped, and Wes told him to read 1 John 1:9. When Terry read that verse, he felt the slipping less and less in his life, and he became a regular child of God. This is what God did for Terry.

That if you confess with your mouth the Lord Jesus and believe in your heart that God raised Him from the dead, you will be saved.

—Romans 10:9

Jay and Meadow: Their best day was the first day when they reconnected in person. After ten years, they had their second first date! They had talked on the phone a few times, but then Meadow had a free day—not common for a single mom and student with a full-time job.

They agreed to meet at the mall, walking three laps around the entire building, talking nonstop, catching up. Still, they did not want to separate, so they went to a midnight movie where they continued to talk, and joke and laugh. They were both a little guarded. Damaged. Scared to hurt each other and scared of becoming hurt. But it was fun. Easy. Comfortable. Refreshing. It was their beginning of "*us*."

Neither one has been perfect. At times, they have

hurt each other but have loved each other and grown, learning how to give one another grace. Meadow is so thankful to walk through life with Jay, and Jay with Meadow.

Michelle: Her first best day was June 1, 1989, the day her daughter was born. Michelle's daughter has continued to make them so proud; she is a wonderful mom to their grandkids! She has chosen a career in education and continues to excel. Michelle and her husband love watching their daughter flourish with everything she puts her mind to.

Angel: Her first best day was the day she had her son. She and her son's dad were living in Lakewood, Colorado, in 2014 when she found out she was pregnant. She was so scared at first! She remembers being in their apartment when she called her son's dad and told him she needed to go buy a pregnancy test; she bought two tests. They were both positive.

At first, she did not want to have the baby, so she set up an appointment at a clinic for an abortion. The morning of the appointment, something did not feel right as soon as she woke up. She had not told anyone she was pregnant. They were driving to the abortion clinic, and she asked Eric, the baby's dad, to pull over.

Eric pulled off the highway and she broke down crying. She had this feeling in the pit of her stomach. She told Eric she did not want to go through with the abortion. They talked and cried together; they both were scared to be parents.

Instead of going to the appointment, they drove to their families' homes to tell them they were going to have a baby. She knew then what God had planned for them.

On March 2, 2015, Angel gave birth to a happy, perfect baby boy. She will never forget looking into his eyes for the first time. It was truly the best day of her life. God chose her to be his mom, and she could not be more grateful and thankful for that!!

She has had a few years of setback and by the grace of God, He is building her up to be the best mom she can be for her son.

Justin: I met Justin at physical therapy. I first noticed him in the waiting room. When the therapist came out to get him, Justin stood up; it was with concentrated effort and quite slow. But he stood up, without assistance of any kind.

Once inside, we had an opportunity to talk while doing our PT, and that is when he told me his best first day was one month before. He woke up from back and neck surgery and knew immediately it was successful! The pain level in his neck and back was zero for pain. Zero. He could not believe it! His pain level before for the previous thirteen years had been an eight...for thirteen years! Now zero! He had been in a wheelchair for the past year.

Justin experienced something when he woke up from surgery that he referred to as being reborn—having peace, incredible appreciation, love for people, even the mean ones, he said. Justin said after the surgery, he woke up in a peaceful state. He said the self-hate dropped off and the self-harm left with it, and he had peace.

Justin has another surgery to undergo, but his outlook is evident when you are in his presence. He is moving forward with his best day.

Regina: Her first best day happened when she was a young teenager. She had attended church her whole life but never truly understood why. She honestly thought most everyone in her small sixty-person congregation was a bit crazy.

That is, until one Sunday when she was singing next to her mother and grandmother in the church choir and watching her pastor's wife do a little jig. Suddenly she was flooded with the most beautiful and intense thoughts and emotions. She was filled with love, joy, thankfulness, hope, excitement, and a host of other feelings and knew it was Christ in her.

Before this, she had never truly appreciated her church or even her family like she did now. Her worship became more than just something that was expected of her. She sang more than a song; she poured out her heart. She felt clean and new. This was her first best day!

***

The first day we opened At Liberty Bookstore was a dream come true from my childhood. My husband and I had worked nonstop, other than Sundays, for several months, getting the store ready to open. My husband's extended gift to me was that he would continue working and I would run the store.

Even before the first customer came in, the Holy Spirit pressed into my heart and said, "Your place here is to embrace *all* people who come in. You don't know how high their walls are or why; I am going to pour an incredible love into your heart with which to love them!"

The first year At Liberty was open, 282 Holy Bibles

were purchased within the small community of three thousand people! This was like rain in the desert.

The store was closed on Sundays and Mondays. One time, I came back in on Tuesday and the door was not locked, it had been unlocked for two days and nights. When I went in, there was nothing out of place. I always said our town was like Mayberry.

***

A customer would stop in often, mostly to talk. When he talked with me, he would get super close to my face. He almost always had perspiration on his face, with pronounced lines on his forehead. He was dealing with post-traumatic stress. It was apparent to me he suffered from anxiety as well. I was not afraid. I understood the symptoms of PTSD.

As our friendship continued to grow, I listened to his story as a wounded warrior, I had compassion for him. I invited him to sit in my office while I transcribed his story.

***

One of my best days at the bookstore happened when an elderly man brought in an item for laminating. As

I laminated his item, I asked him to bring his wife in, who was waiting in the car. He promptly went outside and brought his bride through the door, guiding her with tenderness. She was noticeably frail, in her nineties, and did not appear to have eyesight.

Once inside, she looked up and started turning ever so slowly until she had completed a full circle. She planted her feet and exclaimed in a loud voice, "The Lord is here!" I stood there in amazement! It was a priceless display of faith to witness!

***

As steward of the bookstore, I discovered more about the power of the spoken Word of God. I understood the power of edification by the spoken Word. Now, I gained more understanding of backing the enemy out by the power of the spoken Word!

The first occasion of speaking the Word happened only a few weeks after we opened the bookstore. An older man would come in and try to convince me that I had no faith. I would ignore him until he eventually would leave. He came in several times. On one occasion, he left a cassette on the checkout counter, instructing me to listen to it. As soon as he left, I picked up the cassette with a tissue and threw it in the trash barrel out back.

One day as I was working, he came to the doorway of my office and started spouting his twisted lies regarding the scriptures. I ignored him for a few minutes...then I turned toward him, took one step forward, and said, "Jesus says in Hebrews 13:5, He will never leave nor forsake me." The man took one step back. I advanced again, stating, "God says in Matthew 10:28, no man shall pluck me out of His hand." He had slithered into a position close to the store entrance door; the power of the spoken Word had zipped his lips, and he scurried out, never to come back!

Therefore submit to God. Resist the devil and he will flee from you.

— James 4:7

***

And then there is love. The love of Jesus is pure, the best resting place to be! Early one evening, a couple came into the bookstore. The woman was showing disrespect right away for me and for the store. She swaggered through the store, cursing.

She approached the cash register without a purchase. I asked her, "Where do you all live?"

She sneers and says, "A ways down the road."

I said, "I would like to give you something." She held out her hand, and I placed a store discount card in her hand and told her the next time they came in, they could get a discount.

She started sputtering and stuttering, and they left. The love of Jesus took the wind out of their sails, and they could wreak havoc no more!

**

Accepting people for who they are does not mean agreement. Investing in people does not mean holding them up; that is why they have bootstraps.

Justin, whom I had tutored in the fifth grade and had not seen for five years, told his mom, "We need to find Mrs. Bonnie!" He wanted to be certain I received an invitation for his high school graduation. Following graduation, we all reconnected over pizza. He looked the same, only bigger and with muscles. His heart was certainly the same: kind, gentle, and respectful. It was fun and exciting to listen to his hopes and dreams. It was a day in time to remember for sure!

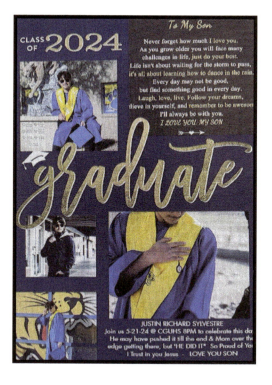

Chapter 7

Pause on Purpose

Timing. Decisions. Stress-Busters.

I was eight years old and had been stealing candy from a little store right up the street where we lived. On this particular day, I stole a bag of candy, and I was waiting outside for my siblings when the store owner came out and asked me what I had behind my back. I gave him the bag of candy, and he asked me for my phone number. I told him we did not have a phone. So *now* I was a liar and a thief.

He then told me he would have to call the police. Well, since my stepdad was a police officer, I suddenly remembered our home phone number!

My mom came and picked me up and paid for the bag of candy. A little while later, she offered me a piece of the candy. I could not take it, because of my guilt that was hanging on the back of my tonsils.

Later, when my stepdad came home, he took me for a ride in his police car and talked to me about stealing and jail time. He took me to a different store that I'd admitted to stealing from. He asked me if there were any other stores from which I had stolen. I admitted there was another one. He took me there and gave me some money to pay and confess to the owner what I had done. This lesson stopped me right in my tracks of the habit of taking something that did not belong to me.

When I was ten years old, one evening our family was enjoying ice cream cones at the dining room table. Two scoops of ice cream. We were talking and laughing as we enjoyed this rare treat. I licked my ice cream and knocked the top scoop off. As quick as lightning, I stuck my elbow out and hit the scoop of ice cream, catapulting it into the air, grabbed it with my hand and threw it in my mouth! We all erupted into uncontrollable belly laughs!

I reacted with lightning speed to rescue the ice cream from falling onto the table because I was savoring it, and I understood there probably was not any more left in the carton!

When I was fifteen years old, I had recently obtained my driver's permit. I was driving our family vehicle with my mom. My mom said, "Bonnie, when we get to the main road, I want you to pull over and I will drive." She was not ready for me to drive at higher speeds. I was a responsible teenager; however, I had a mischievous side also. So when we got to the main road, I stopped at the stop sign, almost rolled through it, and then turned onto the highway. My mom was yelling at me to pull over while I was laughing the whole time.

When I was seventeen years old, I was driving in a new town. There was a red light up ahead of me, and I pulled behind two cars to make a right-hand turn on red. Still a little bit new to driving, I was proud of myself to make this choice of "right on red." No one was making a move, so when the light turned green, I started honking my horn at the two cars ahead of me. Then...I realized I had pulled in behind two parked cars! Shades of red.

When I was eighteen years old, I crawled on my belly to catch a little kitty hiding under a bush. This took some perseverance, but he was worth the effort. It was a young Manx kitty with a bobtail. I named him Cinder because he was jet black. I carried him close to my chest, took him home, and introduced him to Kibi, my calico cat. They bonded immediately.

Cinder never did take to the people who came into the house; he kept tendencies of the wild in his blood. He would run and hide.

Cinder was always lying-in wait for a chance to escape outside. One time, he was gone for more than a day, and I was afraid he had returned to the wild. I eventually found him in the shed and took him inside. Kibi, who had a jealous nature, sniffed him, and then sat up on her back legs and boxed him right in his face with her front paws!

***

Our family was traveling to Glendale, Arizona, to visit Uncle Bob and Aunt Judy. We stopped at a small café on the way for a snack. We entered the café, where there were six barstools at the counter. We hopped onto the stools, taking all six. My mom was standing at the side with a baby on her hip. A Hungarian waitress came out and, with eyes like saucers, said, "Dese kids, they all yours?"

My mom nodded and said, "Yes. I would like six orders of french fries, six glasses of water, and a cup of coffee."

The waitress hollered toward the kitchen, "Da poor lady. Bring her a cup of coffee!"

***

My daughter-in-law was on hyperalert, as her husband was out of town for training. David's cat was a hunter and would carry his "gifts" through the doggie door at night. David's wife was sleeping, and she felt something brushing against her arm. Thinking it was Zeus the cat, she swept it away; then it happened again. She brushed it away again with the thought that if it happened one more time, she was going to turn on the light. That did not take long, and she turned on the light to see Zeus at the corner of the bed with his tail twitching, staring at the kangaroo rat that was on her. She threw the rat off her and hopped out of bed. After a series of "hunting attempts," she was finally able to catch the "gift" Zeus had brought to her, at which point she took it outside and let it go.

***

This joke is about John, a true servant of the Lord. John had a dream one night that the Lord came to him and said, "John, you have been a faithful servant, and I want to reward you with one wish, anything you want."

John looked at the Lord and said, "Well, I have always wanted to go to Hawaii, but I am afraid to fly. Could you build a bridge for me?"

The Lord said, "Yes, that would not be too difficult. I could position the pillars down to the floor of the ocean and build the bridge. But I am surprised at your request; it is not what I would expect from a man like you. I will give you a week to pray about it, and I will come back. If you still want this request, it will be yours. However, you might think of something better."

A week later, the Lord came back and asked John about his wish. John said, "As you know, Lord, I have been married for forty years. I still do not why my wife cries, and her emotions are the most difficult to understand. Lord, could you help me to understand my wife?"

The Lord paused and said, "Do you want two lanes or four lanes on that bridge, John?"

***

At one point in our lives, we had some interesting times due to the family's critters: a Queensland heeler dog, a kitty cat, a bull snake, and an inherited hamster named Fritz from my mom.

I took responsibility for the hamster. When I came in from work one evening, I went in to check Fritz's food and water supply and noticed he was not moving; his eyes were bugged out. He was not dead but was clearly in shock. I asked my husband about him, and Bob said, "I showed him to the dog, and he tried to eat Fritz." Two days later, Fritz came out of shock and lived a full life.

We could not figure out how Fritz was escaping from his cage on top of a chest of drawers and roaming the house. He would stop by the cat food bowl and pack in some cat food on his way behind the dryer, tear up the dryer hose, and nest. Fritz would often journey into the bathroom and hide in a small space under the sink cabinet.

Finally, we found out the answer to Fritz's mode of escape. I was in the room when Fritz opened the door of his cage, scurried over to the edge of the dresser top, and peered into the crack between the dresser and the wall. I said, "No, Fritz, you will hurt yourself." He dove into the crack, slid down about six inches, and then puffed out to stop himself; he repeated this process until he landed onto the floor. I nicknamed Fritz's maneuver "the elevator ride," and anyone who came into the house was invited to come and see it. It might sound kind of silly, but it was quite amazing to witness. We call that "cheap entertainment," something our family was pretty good at—which, of course, was hereditary.

***

My husband and son Ben were on a bicycle outing when Ben saw a bull snake in the road. Bob picked it up and was going to release it in the desert when Ben spoke up. "Bob, this is a perfectly good snake!"

They decided to bring the bull snake home and set up an aquarium after reading a book from the local library on how to care for a snake in captivity. The book read, "Do not expect affection from your snake." Most people would salute that idea, but my husband proved the book wrong. If Bob had the snake and anyone would try to take it, Jake would wrap around Bob's forearm and hold on. If someone else had the snake, Bob could hold his hand out, and Jake would slither on over to be with Bob!

We soon learned that the best and most economical way to feed Jake was to hunt for lizards, which were not hard to find; it was fun to do. There was no brick-and-mortar store, but we knew a little bit about "God's reptile shop," a.k.a. the desert.

One time, there was an exceptionally big lizard in the aquarium with Jake. The lizard had Jake's head in its mouth and appeared to be interested in trying snake for dinner. There was a family dinner discussion as to whether Jake needed a rescue from the lizard. It was decided the lizard appeared to be winning, so Bob got up from the table and stabbed the lizard with his fork and guts spilled out of the lizard. Honestly, I do not think too much fazed us either—a lot like Grandma Pat.

***

This joke is about when Forrest Gump went to heaven.

Saint Peter met him at the gate and said, "OK, Forrest, you have to pass a quiz to get into heaven."

Forrest replied, "Oh, do not make it too hard. I had a pretty hard time already on earth."

"How many days of the week start with the letter *T*?"

"That is easy, two! Today and tomorrow!"

"Well, that is not what we had in mind, but we will take it." Then Saint Peter said, "How many seconds are in a year?"

Forrest thought for a minute, and then he said, "Twelve!"

"How do you get twelve?"

"You know...January second, February second, March second..."

"OK," Peter replied. Then Peter asked, "What is the first name of God?"

"That is easy, Andy!"

"Andy?"

And Forrest started singing. "Yes. *And He* walks with me, *and He* talks with me!"

Saint Peter opened the Heaven's gate and said, "Run, Forrest, run!"

Chapter 8

Freedom

Way. Patriot. Military.

Integrity with Liberty
Editor, Bonnie Haak

I believe we are so fortunate to live in the land of the free...the home of the brave. We should be mindful to remember the sacrifices of those who have stood firm with courage and conviction in serving and protecting our country.

I agree with the mindset that I have a duty to do my part as a citizen of the community, as a citizen of the United States of America to benefit my fellow mankind. And I will be ever grateful that I can...because of those places that have been steadfastly and courageously declared and protected for my freedom.

My most humble adoration and thanks.

***

When I was steward of At Liberty, it was a time to organize sending prayer cards and supplies overseas for our military serving overseas.

In this endeavor, four local churches banded together, eager to participate in sending supplies and prayer cards to show their love and support for our military. The response was so great in the community, as supplies were donated, and prayer cards were written and brought to the At Liberty bookstore and in addition to our home residence.

A total of 225 pounds was sent over to our soldiers because of our freedom to purchase, write, and mail these supplies. The land of the free because of the brave!

***

The day I was born a female *and* blessed to be inside a country of *freedom* happened on the day of my birth in the United States of America! I had a keen sense, even when I was little, regarding my freedom and the cost, not to take that lightly. And today I continue with a patriotic heart and a deep gratitude for our military; past, present, and future.

***

The first day when I became a born-again Christian, I was twenty-seven years old. I found a freedom I had never known before. The freedom from carrying the burden of my sins: guilt, shame, and regrets. A freedom to forgive myself and others. Freedom to embrace my new desires given by the leading of the gift of the Holy Spirit, the Helper.

David enjoying a day out, a pause for sure!

My crazy mom, never a dull moment!

Ma Beavers baked her special "Beaver Bars" by the hundreds and other goodies to take to the mine site where she worked as a security guard.

"Ma" was presented with a glass "Merry Christmas" plaque with eighty-three coworkers' names inscribed on the back. Included in their gift was a KitchenAid mixer! She did not expect this outpouring of love, but those miners were so thankful to be able to show their appreciation.

As much as Mom loved to bake, the card meant much more to her than the mixer.

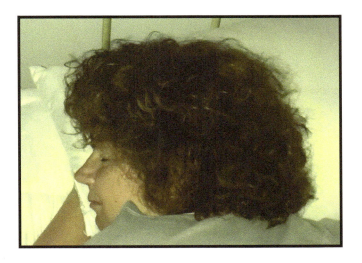

Thank you, US armed forces and First responders, and to my parents for teaching me faith, family, and freedom!

Part Two

Testimonies

A gift of wood artwork for my 60th birthday from Ben and his family. The design was specified by Ben and created by Ben's friend and fellow veteran.

Chapter 9

Opportunities

Stop. Pray. Discern.

Sister-in-Christ Marci, evangelist and prayer warrior. Marci continues onward, stepping for Jesus, having celebrated her one hundredth birthday this year!

I met CJ in the hospital. I affectionately called her CJ because she had a degree in criminal justice. We were sitting together talking, and we were discussing spiritual belief, specifically belief in God. I was going to quote a verse to her, but the verse I knew by heart for many years was not coming to my mind.

CJ said, "That is OK; there is a Bible right over there." She walked over to the table and picked it up, and asked me, "What verse did you say it was?"

I responded, "John 3:16."

She sat down with the Bible open and read the verse aloud. Immediately following, she believed in Jesus as God's Son and in God's plan for her life. CJ was forty-three years old.

After discharge from the hospital, my husband and I were able to purchase a Bible for CJ and a bouquet of paper flowers with the verse 1 John 4:19 on each one.

We traveled back to the hospital and parked by the outside fenced area. I slipped CJ's Bible through the gate opening, which fortunately was big enough.

As the paper flowers with the scripture verse were shared among the people who were outside smoking cigarettes, the place came alive! People were jumping for joy, laughing, and crying upon receiving this gift of the Word from Jesus!

For God so loved the world that He gave His Only Begotten Son. that whoever believes in Him should not perish but have everlasting life. For God did not send His Son into the world to condemn the world, but that the world through Him might be saved.

—John 3:16–17

***

My husband and I were in the garage at our home when a young man, twenty-nine years old, without a shirt or shoes on, came walking by. I asked him his name, and we sat down on the curb by the pavement. It was clear he was troubled, and so I asked him a few questions. Pretty soon, I asked him, "Are you a Christian?"

He responded, "People say I am."

"Do you know what it means to be a Christian?"

"No, not really."

I gave him a homemade burrito; he received it gratefully. I started telling him all about Jesus; he hung his head, and the tears started rolling down his cheeks as he listened.

Bill and Joann, Awana leaders, were generous with their time, finances, and resources. He would say to me, "Bonnie, you cannot outgive God."

Bill was a great encouragement to me in Awana, and I appreciated his frankness as well. His focus was for people to know the Truth, and he purposefully posted in different areas and communities for those opportunities as God opened them.

Bill had a prayerful heart. I mentioned to Pastor David about Bill's prayerful heart, and our pastor said, "Oh, really? He has a Purple Heart?' Well, my enunciation is not always great; however, I do believe Bill has a Purple Heart now, as he walks and talks with his Savior.

This page is dedicated to my brother-in-Christ Bill, an evangelist, who bought Bibles *by the case* to share the promises of God!

Not by works of righteousness which we have done, but according to His mercy He saved us, through the washing of regeneration and renewing of the Holy Spirit,
—Titus 3:5

Love you, Joann!

This best day happened when I was approaching the entrance of a retail store in Casa Grande, and there was a young man, eighteen years old, at a table with information for bullying prevention. I stopped and talked with him and asked questions, including if he was a Christian. He said, "Yes, I am a Christian, but I have been drifting away from my faith."

I always carry a New Testament in my purse. I gave him the NT, along with some snacks, and his face lit up as he opened the Bible. The Bible has the answer for backing the Bully out; he has to flee!

***

I was standing in the customer service line at a large retail store when an older man started bellowing, "Where is the manager?"

I thought to myself, "he is angry."

The manager came, and the man and I were right next to each other as the associates took care of our returns. I could hear the man talking to the manager, whom he had previously spoken with regarding his product return. He asked her, "Do I have the right container of lettuce now?" His voice was gentle, and I sensed kindness.

When I stepped away, I waited for him and asked, "Are you God's man?"

He asked, "What?"

I repeated my question. He lowered his thick, dark glasses and looked toward me. He was blind! He lifted a cross off his neck and held it out for me to see.

I said, "You have such an authoritative and powerful voice, and you should keep using it for God."

Glasses still lowered, his eyes filled with tears, and with a choked voice, he said, "You have no idea the struggle I have been going through. He sent you in here to encourage me today!"

**

The day I went to work at the senior citizens' center was exciting and challenging too. I met a coworker on the first day where we would share office space together. He had a habit of taking the Lord's name in vain. He would cuss, and I would silently pray like Jesus: "Father, forgive him for he knows not what he does." Floyd stopped cussing a few months later. We were becoming friends. He had a gruff exterior and an alcohol dependence, but I could see he was a lot softer on the inside than one would expect.

Floyd was seventy years old, and he became open

to Christianity. No, we did not really talk about it at work on the boss's dime. We didn't, but the Holy Spirit did!

Floyd's heart was becoming more and more open, so one day as we were coming into work, I stopped him outside. I said, "Floyd, you have already seen how God has put you on my heart, and you need to know some things." He had his head down, looking at the sidewalk. Filled with the leading of the Holy Spirit, I said, "You will go to heaven or hell, and you need to decide if you believe in Jesus as God's one and only Son, who died on the cross for you and for me, was buried, and rose again on the third day. I am here to tell you, He is real, and He loves you! If you can believe in Him *and* ask Him to forgive you, then you will become a child of God with the promise of an eternity in Heaven."

Floyd slowly looked up with tears swimming in his eyes and said, "Bonnie, I am going to go home this weekend and read the Bible and think about this."

When I saw Floyd the following week, I knew right away that he had made his decision for Christ. His countenance and even his posture had changed! I approached him and asked him, "Do you know what happened when you believed in Jesus?"

Floyd said, "No."

I laid my hand on his heart and said, "The Holy Spirit landed right there."

He wept.

***

We were having a staff meeting in the office at the senior citizens' center where I worked when the assistant manager proceeded to chastise me for having a Bible at work, which was interesting because there were Bibles in the building. As she continued to berate me in front of everyone, I felt the back of my neck getting hot. Then the Spirit calmed me and brought peace back into my heart.

The next day, I came to work with a beautiful white flower I had purchased for the assistant manager. I was known for being straightforward. She looked at me as I approached her desk with the flower. I placed the flower on her desk, and before I even spoke, her eyes started filling with tears. Enough said.

***

One day as my husband and I drove down the street, we noticed a hole in the rear window of our van. We had been taking care of my husband's parents' house, and across the street there was a family with six children. They were a rowdy bunch. We decided the damage to our window came from these neighborhood kids, but we had no proof.

I told Bob, "I know what to do. Let's make burritos." He agreed. We made two dozen burritos and took them over to the neighbors. The problems that seemed to be simmering stopped. We never had any kind of trouble with the neighbors, their kids, their noise level, or their pit bulls after that.

***

I was asked by the director of a Christian school to serve as a Bible teacher for the high school girls. I encouraged the young ladies to open their Bible, always checking the "message" against the text: "Any pastor worth his salt will be glad you are."

While I was at the school campus, I was asked to narrate Holy Week. I am not sure if I understood that request, but I understood, with the Spirit's leading, that I wanted to give the students an opportunity for a drama. So I wrote a four-part drama for Holy Week and asked my brother-in-Christ Chuck to be the narrator.

We started with Palm Sunday, when I invited the

students to be a part of the crowd, waving palm leaves and greeting Jesus with hallelujahs. They eagerly accepted. When I asked for someone to portray Jesus, riding into Jerusalem on a donkey, a sixteen-year-old young man jumped up and imitated riding a donkey while he whipped it to go faster. I chuckled and said, "Jesus does not whip the donkey." So we forged ahead with the first scene of Holy Week.

When we prepared for Maundy Thursday, the Last Supper, I was able to purchase beautiful blue wine goblets from the dollar store. There was no lack of participation of twelve young men when I explained that we would be having homemade bread at the table. The staff from the local newspaper office showed up to take a picture of our portrayal of the Last Supper.

When we were preparing for the Good Friday, I opted for a message regarding how it was my sin, our sin, that nailed Jesus to the Cross. A time of reflection on His Crucifixion.

Preparing for the fourth part was amazing: the resurrection of Jesus Christ! We had an open invitation to the local community.

Pastor Robert Cox, the school chaplain, brought the message on Easter Sunday.

Resurrection Day Sermon, April 2007

When was the last time that you got in trouble. Did you call upon the name of Jesus? In chapter 8 of the gospel of John, you will find in this passage that Jesus came also for those who are outcasts by this world's standards. Hallelujah!
Jesus came as Savior of the whole world for anyone who would believe in His name!
Pastor Cox reminded the congregation that we had come that day seeking the truth—to find the Truth. It is not about the preacher's preaching, it is not about the deacon's prayer, it is not about the choir singing or about the Easter Bunny or egg hunting. It is about finding out that Jesus is who He says He is, and that can He do what He says He can do.
A good Shepherd knows His sheep.
He came to lay down His life for Jews and Gentiles. Too many people want to hear from somebody else what is going on, instead of going to see for themselves. According to God's Word, we need to be Bereans, studiers of the Word. When the people heard Jesus had raised Lazarus from the dead, they went to see for themselves if this was true.
One has to die to his own ways in order to become fruitful in God's ways. Unless we die to our

old ways, we cannot see the kingdom of God.
Jesus's victory was on the Cross!
This sermon on Easter Day is a Sermon that we
should be concerned about each and every day, to
know what Jesus has done for us. He is alive!

And you shall know the truth, and the truth shall
make you free.

—John 8:32

The room was packed. The waiting congregation was diverse, from various local churches and community citizens. At the end of Pastor Cox's sermon, everyone in the room sat still and made no attempt to get out of their seats! The Holy Spirit was permeating the whole room with His presence.

***

A local pastor's wife invited me to organize a women's mentoring ministry. This was yet another opportunity for interdenominational encouragement and unity of the Spirit. Our mentoring materials were given to like-faith pastors to review and approve.

Subsequently, the next two years of meeting in homes for mentoring, singing, Bible reading, and much more...is a book in itself. What we can learn from one another should never be neglected. In unity, there are no denominations. The same Spirit speaks to each of one of us in the name of Jesus!

***

And as Pastor Corley proclaimed, "There is a day coming where you will want to know your brother or sister in the street, so we better get busy doing that now!" He made this statement during "church in the park" one Sunday where ten churches came together and lifted praises and prayer to the heavens, followed by food and fellowship!

***

Years before, I found myself united with, Charlene, a sister-in-Christ for "breaking down some walls:" Racial walls, legalistic walls, socioeconomic walls within the church. The Holy Spirit is not limited to what He will do in a broken and willing vessel.

***

Another notable blessing was when my husband and I attended a monthly prayer meeting that included seven area churches. God's people, in unity of the Spirit, praying and singing for an hour. We would rotate through the participating churches. The vision for interdenominational prayer was given to our pastor, Marty, blessed by Jesus with serious prayer warriors and the beautiful voices of those with the gifting of song. This was rich, so rich that my husband and I attended the first Monday of every month for eight years before moving to Arizona.

***

Looking back at it now, I can appreciate that I grew up in a family of "includers." In God's greater plan, He was working in my heart for unity, for interdenominational support and ministries, for the simplicity of His gospel and to love all people in His name with the help of the Holy Spirit. God does not call the qualified; He qualifies the *called*.

Grandson Matthew

Chapter 10
Before Words, Afterwards

Decision. Forgiveness. Hope.

The first day I believed in God led me to an understanding that His plan for me is to have a relationship with Him. I understood because He showed me; He sent Jesus, His one and only Son because of His love for me. This was beyond my comprehension, yet the depths of my heart told me it was true. His one and only Son! *Who does that?*

Jesus forgave my sins and took my burdens and regrets in exchange for peace in my heart! At the moment of believing, the Holy Spirit entered my heart where He leads, convicts, warns, protects, comforts, and gives power and authority over the enemy of my soul, by the name of Jesus! At age twenty-seven, I understood the needed Helper in navigating my life.

***

The first day my brother Eddie woke up from an induced coma for which major surgery was performed, and I spoke with him on the phone, I had to hand my husband the phone. I was overcome because Eddie's voice was so familiar and strong! I was overcome with gratitude.

Ten days before, Eddie had been on his way to buy some drugs, and the car he was riding in was T-boned by an oncoming car. The doctor stated that only fifteen percent of patients survive the types of injuries my brother suffered!

When my husband handed the phone back to me, I said to my brother, "Eddie, God saved you from a physical death to give you a spiritual life. Do you want to know how to become a Christian?"

He immediately said, "Yes." Eddie believed from his heart in Jesus that day.

If He leads you to it, He will bring you through it. On a yes.

Eddie's recovery from the accident was significantly quicker than what the doctors predicted. He was told he would be in a wheelchair and would not walk for a year; he was out of the wheelchair and on his feet in three months! Eddie knew in his heart God was restoring him.

When Eddie was discharged from the hospital a

few months after the accident, our sister drove to Phoenix to take him to her home in Tucson. She took him to church and his numerous follow-up medical appointments; she stayed in prayer, kept his medications straight, and tirelessly looked after him as he continued to heal.

My sister contacted me to ask if I could travel to Tucson to look after our brother while she and her husband went on vacation. During the time I was in their home, my brother and I had a season for uninterrupted conversations! This was a time of healing in more ways than one.

Eddie explained to me then that when he woke up from his ten-day coma, he knew right away "something" was different. He could not place it, but he knew it was real. He recognized later that "something" was God giving him a spiritual life and a second chance!

Through an opportunity at his church, Eddie joined a team to restore a Volkswagen Bug, and continued to grow in his faith. Soon after, Eddie was hired as a car mechanic. Howard, an eighty-three-year-old prayer warrior would stop by Eddie's work weekly to ask my brother if he would like prayer. Eddie told me, "Bonnie, everything I ask Howard to pray for gets answered!"

Eddie was not only restored from the injuries from

the accident, but he was restored in his relationships as well. He was forty years old at the time of his accident, and his deepest desires were for marriage and a family.

The woman he had dated and partied hard with prior to the accident took notice of the transformation in his life, and she realized she, too, needed Jesus. She had three children from a previous marriage.

Eddie and his wife embraced Christian counseling, including abstaining from sex outside of marriage. They were married in 2009 at their church. This was Eddie's ultimate dream in life!

Eddie and his wife had three more children, and with open arms, he embraced the role of being a dad to all six children!

***

I was serving as a food ministry coordinator at a local church, when a twenty-year-old man came into the food pantry, leaving his grocery cart parked outside.

His name was Salvador, and he talked with me regarding his present situation. He had aged out of foster care at eighteen. He had never been in possession of his birth certificate, which of course hindered him in obtaining a driver's license and affected him in getting gainful employment. People only know what they know, until they know different. I collected food items for him as we visited, and he accepted a Bible because he wanted to learn more about God.

Once we were outside, he reached for a can of soup, opened the pop-top, tilted his head back, and poured it down his throat. I stopped to wait for him, and he told me that this was the first he had eaten for three days. I swallowed hard, embarrassed about having had concern for him chugging it without the added can of water mixed in. *And I became keenly aware of his need to survive even beyond the point of getting food for a day.*

My husband and I cooked some steaks and decided to take dinner to Salvador. We scouted the area where he said he was staying but could not find him.

The next evening my friend Debby and I were driving in the area, looking for Salvador, and we saw him enter a grocery store. We parked and started for the entrance of the store when a young woman near the store entrance grabbed my arm as I was walking by and said, "My husband is going to steal some food because we are so hungry, but I do not want him to get arrested." Recognizing this was a divine appointment, we entered the store and saw Salvador at the cash register talking to the clerk. When he saw me, he came over and explained he had not taken anything but was asking the store clerk a question. I let out a sigh of relief and asked him if we could take him and his wife, Mia, to dinner. He gratefully accepted.

They attended church the next Sunday and took the opportunity to meet with the pastor. Mia had traveled from a neighboring city to find Salvador while an aunt took care of their baby girl. They had made some mistakes, and there had been an intervention in their young family for the baby's welfare.

I encouraged them to attend the gathering of churches with praise and worship scheduled at a local park for that Sunday afternoon. Their hearts had become open to the truths of God and their need to give Him their lives, and right there in the park that afternoon, they became Christians. Soon afterward, they returned home, reconciled to God and with each other.

Heather: Her best day was February 21, 1994. The reason is...it was the day she *truly* met Jesus!

She had grown up in the church; baptized at age eleven. She knew about Jesus and felt she knew the difference between right and wrong.

While growing up, Heather experienced the pain of her parents' divorce; subsequently, she found her value in the attention of boyfriends. This led to numerous relationships—toxic relationships—because she did not want to be alone.

Heather moved to Kentucky to escape a relationship with a boyfriend. It was there, at the University of Kentucky, where she was invited by a friend to Campus Crusade for Christ and to church. In the process of getting more involved in both, she broke up with her boyfriend. She continued choosing more faith-based activities.

Heather did not realize it at the time, but God was continually drawing her near to Him, to cause her to seek more of Him. She had a hole in her heart that could only be filled by Jesus. She had spent way too much time trying to fill it with men and their attention.

After weeks of attending church with her best friend Julie, it happened: the *best moment* of Heather's life!

All her life, up to this moment, Heather thought she was a Christian. Come to find out, she was trying to be a good enough person to make it into Heaven.

One day she met with her pastor's wife. Subsequently, Heather, at twenty-two years of age, accepted it is by faith to believe in Jesus with her heart, ask His forgiveness for her sins, and choose to live for Him.

The realization that she was created for a purpose,

for this time in history, settled into her heart. And now she has peace in the middle of the storms of life.

God's peace during pregnancy: Four out five of Heather's pregnancies were high risk; in one of her pregnancies, the doctor thought her baby might die in utero. Heather chose prayer and trusted in God in the face of this news about her baby, whatever the outcome. Peace filled her heart, leaving no room for fear. Fortunately, the baby survived and is now a six-foot-four young man in good health! Heather's trust and faith made an incredible difference for her during a time of uncertainty.

Years later, married for seventeen years and with five kids, she found herself divorced. Her résumé at this point in her life was a stay-at-home mom who had homeschooled her five kids.

God provided! A few years later, she went back to nursing school as a single mama with five kids and graduated with an associate of science in nursing.

She thought nursing would be perfect! Three twelve-hour shifts a week would work for her family. Nursing unfortunately, left her feeling exhausted and burned out. Yet it was then that Heather realized God had something better: Health coaching! Little did she know that entrepreneurship would become a part of her life.

Never, ever did Heather think God would call her out of the hospital to serve people as an optimal health and well-being transformation coach, but without doubt, He did. As she stood by the bedsides of her patients with lifestyle-related issues, she felt her heart ache and knew her place of calling was to help people create health rather than manage sickness. She resigned from the hospital, responded to God's call, and became a health coach.

Heather recognizes that she would not be where she is today, nor would her family be who they are today but only because of the saving grace of Jesus. Nor would she have endured the valleys of life with gratitude over grumbling, worship over worry, faith over fear!

This is how Heather came to the place in her life where she *truly* met and developed a personal, intimate, transforming relationship with Christ and why it was the best day of her life.

Joshua: His first best day started by letting go of all the negative things in the world when he became a born-again Christian at age twenty-seven. He let go of the negative and started embracing hope and what God says about him and anxiety.

Cast your burden on the LORD, And He shall sustain you; He shall never permit the righteous to be moved.

—Psalm 55:22

Joshua had experienced a lot of trauma in his life. Doctors diagnosed him with anxiety and depression. He used to smoke, drink, and put his faith in other things, using them as a crutch or security blanket. But nothing he did would satisfy or heal what was really going on in his life. He learned to let go and let God. His spirit and mind were made new. He found that with being filled with the Holy Spirit daily, there was no room for anxiety, depression, or negative thoughts because his focus was on what God says about him, and His promises are for him.

Joshua believes everyone has a story and we all go through struggles and hardships. He believes if everyone does their part to spread the light to people we encounter, we can face anything; we never know the impact we can make with our testimony!

Angel: She was once dead because of her failures and sins; she was lost and broken, fearing God for the wrong reasons. She followed the desires of her corrupt nature until she decided to call upon Jesus to change and accept the free gift of God.

She found herself accepting by faith in Jesus Christ. She knew God had a better plan for her, way better than her own. She felt at peace. God restored her identity, faith, family, and the broken relationship she had with her own mother.

She can talk with her family and friends of the Good News, all because her God the Father gave His only begotten Son for her wicked ways. Now she has insight and clarity. Thank you, God.

Jean: Her best day encompasses four seasons of her life. In her first season with Jesus, she was six years old in a primary Sunday school class and remembers realizing she was lost. The answer was to accept Jesus as her personal Savior.

Three years later, her next season started with her accepting Jesus into her heart and being baptized.

She started in another season of walking with Jesus when He pressed into her heart about using her music gift for His glory.

Currently, Jean is in a season of understanding what God's purpose was and is for her life: to share the Gospel with others, and to use everything in her life to glorify Him.

Has she attained perfection? Definitely not...she has failed many times. But the journey has been wonderful, and she has His peace as she walks in the path He has planned for her. Then that is most important to the Father until He calls her home into heaven! Now at eighty years old, she is truly content as never before.

Leila: She said her best day was when she was twenty-one years old; one Saturday night, Jesus spoke to her heart and told her that she was lost, that she was troubled with the cares of life, and she was broken. The next morning, she went to the altar at her church, admitted she was a sinner, needed to be rescued, and that she could not find her way on her own. She was baptized on the same day.

She has learned throughout her lifetime what it takes to walk with Him, reading His Word, and listening in her heart to the Holy Spirit! She does not always obey when He speaks, but she is growing in her faith-walk with the Lord, and she is on a journey. She is going somewhere, and that place she is going to is Heaven, because Jesus has promised her an eternal place in Heaven. Praise Him!

Chapter 11

Keeping It Real

Awareness. Discernment. Education.

This chapter is dedicated to people with mental health challenges and their family members and friends. And it is written with extended love, compassion, and thankfulness for those who serve in the professions of police, fire, clergy, and health practices—any and all who would consider this author's take regarding mental health and mental illness.

Gaining momentum in the areas of education and understanding mental illness can bring healing and compassion; this move also makes the bully livid.

But he does not have to win.

I do not feel like I have all the answers, but I do believe if there is *one thing, just one thing here that will bring some light into a family's struggle with mental health challenges, awesome!* All I am asking for is a chance to do that, having walked in the shoes and the path of mental health challenges for more than thirty years.

I am writing from the standpoint of my own personal experiences and encounters. Although great strides have been made in the past couple of decades regarding mental illness, it continues to carry a stigma.

It is my personal belief the roots of stigma stem from ignorance: a lack of knowledge of the trusted and readily available resources regarding mental health and mental illness. Refer to the back of this book for a list of resources.

Mental illness is hard—no...it is *tremendously* hard during those symptomatic periods for the person with the illness and for their family and friends.

In my personal experience, I support the fact that *although mental illness is real, it does not define a person.*

***

Mental illness can be complicated. The brain is by far the most complex of the body's major organs. Medications for various illnesses—diabetes, heart disease, lung disease—can be effective for treatment of those illnesses and are considered valid. There is an almost universal acceptance by others regarding disease of the body's other major organs. Yet mental illness, which affects the brain, continues to carry a stigma.

***

I believe there are two different kinds of mental illness: diagnosed and undiagnosed. This is not to imply that everyone has mental illness.

By my observation, people opt out of seeking professional help for their symptoms, sometimes because of denial, based on fear of the stigma, or a lack of awareness regarding the illness. Or sometimes they try different avenues of managing their health care on their own.

For mental health care, an individual has a right to choose, *as it should be*.

With those who are diagnosed and choose counseling and medication, they can still become symptomatic. However, their quality of life *overall* can be much improved with mental health treatment. I learned with decisions for medication, *any kind of medication*, to agree with "weigh the risks with the benefits." Of course, that is always a personal choice.

***

Through the years, I have noticed the innate character of a person to be central as to how they will survive with a mental illness—or any illness, for that matter. When a person is "out of character," as you or the family normally know them, this would be something worthy to note.

Please.

When people do not feel well, grace is truly a gift that can be given.

People who have mental illness can be funny, loving, intelligent, creative, kind, compassionate, insightful, sensitive, strong in faith, and so forth. In the case of these type of personality traits, it can be more difficult for an understanding then when a person is "out of character."

My understanding through research is that childhood trauma, abuse, head injury, genetics, trauma, and drugs (including alcohol and prescription drug abuse) can be the cause of mental illness.

***

In my personal experience, *learning* about the effects of childhood trauma, head injury, genetics, trauma, and alcohol dependence relative to the onset of my mental illness brought me to the doorstep to regain my emotional and mental health. It seems pretty simple, but rest assured, it is not. For me, an awareness of the cause of my mental illness took a long time.

A really long time.

Repeated verbal, emotional, physical, and relational abuse can cause trauma. This is bully behavior. I believe writing this chapter has its place in calling the bully out!

When I came to the place in understanding the root cause of my mental illness, I experienced healing to the point where I sat down in total awe! I sat down for half a day.

***

Would you come to the Plate with me? This takes a minute, yet it is so powerful and, I believe, God-given to me for a better understanding of mental illness. Here is the Plate. Hold out your arms and clasp your hands together as if you are holding a dinner plate.

On this Plate are depression, anxiety, posttraumatic stress, attention deficit and hyperactivity, bipolar, schizophrenia, borderline personality, posttraumatic stress, and more.

Everything on this plate has one thing in common: each one affects the major organ, the brain.

Look down at the Plate. Which one would you choose to pick up and put in your brain?

***

My learning curve at this point in my life—and I pray for continuous learning to further shape my future best days—goes back to loving my fellow man enough to take a closer look.

For me, "keeping it real" is my choice of statement for where I hope to see mental health evolving more and more: Awareness. Education. Discernment.

For all parties, whoever those involved parties are.

**

I was twenty-one years old when I made an inner vow following a traumatic event one Christmas Eve night.

As I sat in the middle of my bed, grappling to deal with all of it, I said to myself over and over, "I will never say anything again, no matter how bad it hurts." *I did not know what an inner vow was and that I had just made one.* Unfortunately, I carried that vow for the next seven years, rarely speaking about my feelings. My conversations were held to a surface level only.

The result was I had a serious collapse mentally, emotionally, and physically. It took ten months for my recovery. Once I came to an understanding of what I had done in making the inner vow, it was my first step for healing from the damage it caused me.

My understanding of an inner vow is that it is a personal decision to protect the heart and mind from pain. It can involve words like "always" and "never."

People only know what they know, until they know different.

Trials will do one of three things:
1. Define you
2. Strengthen you
3. Destroy you

Potential Coping Strategies

In the case you are living with someone who suffers with mental illness, try to be as unconditional as you know how. There might be few family/friends who can do this. The good news: that is enough.

- Keep faith practices in place.
- Consistent sleep schedule, experts agree this is paramount. A sleep diary is helpful.
- Consider medication. Weigh the risks and benefits.
- Consider professional counseling.
- Ask if they would like prayer if you pray.
- Enlist deep breathing techniques to relieve tension.

- Eat ice cream.
- Education helps with how to respond to your loved one; it can ease fears and helps communication.
- Have a trusted friend(s) to call who agree to be a support.
- Identify and place healthy boundaries.
- Plan for consistent outlets for fun and relaxation.
- Take downtime with family.
- Help your family and ask for help from them.
- Follow a nutritious food plan and add in daily exercise/stretching.
- Keep a low-stress home and work environment.
- Allow for personal space.
- Be sure to take care of yourself first as a caregiver. If you start becoming embroiled with your loved one's illness, it might be time to step back and sometimes to step out for a little while.

Chapter 12

Champions for Jesus

Perffectionism Is a Trap

We had a ministry in our home for three years, Champions for Jesus, a ministry for children, ages five through fifteen, in preparing and presenting the Gospel through drama and song. Our ministry team included five adults who had a big heart for children, ready to bring their time, spiritual gifts, and joy.

Our ministry would start with a circle of prayer and reading from the Bible, followed by songs, a leisurely hour-long lunch with laughter, conversation, and observation. The children would clear off the tables, and then we would practice drama and songs for the next hour.

At the time, I was forty-eight years old, and the Lord had impressed upon me how important it is to allow children opportunity—to not do everything for them, but to trust children with a belief they will eagerly do something when the door is opened for them. And they did! I would ask for two volunteers to serve lunch to the others (an average of eleven kids), and they would start raising their hands: "Me, me, me!"

The "Whole Armor of God" portrayal was their first choice for a drama presentation. The champions created their whole armor with help from my husband and the team.

The "belt of truth" emerged with a strip of white cloth; they wrote "Truth" on it and tied it around their waists.

"The breastplate of righteousness" was their red shirt.

They attached paper to their shoes with their written word "Peace" for the "preparation of the gospel of peace."

Their cardboard cutouts of the "shield of faith" were covered with tin foil.

Additionally, tin foil worked to create their "helmet of salvation."

"The sword of the Spirit"—their personal Bible— was carried in their hand.

We would practice for the "Whole Armor of God" drama in anticipation for invitations to perform, which subsequently came from three churches in the community. Now the Champions for Jesus were prepared. It was their time to put their drama into action, and they did.

In our town, we would have an Armed Forces Day parade every year. Champions for Jesus and the team built a float for the big day parade.

When the children jumped off their float with great excitement and even greater smiles to perform the "whole armor of God" for the judges and many bystanders, it was a moment in time to remember.

Additionally, the Champions for Jesus visited the local hospital as well as the senior center, where they continually shared the Gospel through their love for Jesus.

It is pretty hard to pick out the best day of those three years, but I would have to say it happened on one occasion when our Champions for Jesus visited the nursing home to offer hugs and the gift of time, and to sing songs for the patients.

Well, there we were at the hospital, and there was an old man who had dementia. He raised his hand in the air, which had only three fingers, and he shook it and said in an angry voice, "You kids, you see this? If you do not behave, this will happen to you!" My immediate reaction was upset, even alarm, when one of our boys, all of six years old, walked over to the man, laid his small hands on the man's leg, and started praying for him. The man visibly relaxed in every sense of the word. I stood there, with tears on my face and in my heart at the power of prayer and the love of a little boy breaking through the anger, confusion, and fears of this man to touch his heart place with love and peace.

While at the hospital, the Champions for Jesus and members of the team would crowd into the room around the bed of a thirty-year-old patient, James, who was in a coma due to a snowboarding accident. I would ask James if he would like us to pray for him. *In that still moment*, he would give us permission by a tear peeking out of the corner of his eye or a faint attempt to smile.

We would sing to him and pray for him. The children, unlike a lot of adults, had no hesitation in getting physically and emotionally close to James. They were not afraid.

The Whole Armor of God:

Finally, my brethren, be strong in the Lord and in the power of His might. Put on the whole armor of God, that you may be able to stand against the wiles of the devil. For we do not wrestle against flesh and blood, but against principalities, against powers, against the rulers of the darkness of this age, against spiritual hosts of wickedness in the heavenly places.

Therefore take up the whole armor of God, that you may be able to withstand in the evil day, and having done all, to stand. Stand therefore, having girded your waist with truth, having put on the breastplate of righteousness, and having shod your feet with the preparation of the gospel of peace; above all, taking the shield of faith with which you will be able to quench all the fiery darts of the wicked one. And take the helmet of salvation, and the sword of the Spirit, which is the word of God;

praying always with all prayer and supplication in the Spirit, being watchful to this end with all perseverance and supplication for all the saints

—Ephesians 6:10-18

Chapter 13

Praise and Prayer

Dwelling Place. Power. Conversation.

This chapter is dedicated to true prayer warriors—who are not eloquent in words or length necessarily, but for those who praise and pray in the Spirit from their hearts to the Most High, like children. Because we know we are His children, and He has anointed us to be His prayer warriors.

***

Written prayers taken directly from her prayer journal:

McKenzie: Date: Unknown. Saturday @ 9:22 p.m. Dear God, I have been here for two days, and I absolutely noticed some C.H.A.N.G.E. occurring and I am beyond grateful! Always will be!

I thank You for giving me this opportunity...not just for myself...but for my family!

I pray that You redirect my thoughts! I also pray and will continue to pray for patience in my life.

I pray for my loved ones...I pray for healing, forgiveness, along with protection...I pray for guidance...I also pray for peace.

I pray for my babies to feel better and to continue to grow healthy.

In Jesus Name, Amen!

Date: Unknown. Sunday @ 9:41 p.m.

Dear God, I have noticed...lately when I do pray...

I have been praying about one specific thing lately...

I have been praying about more patience...

Now when I do pray...

It is usually not specific...

Someone once told me when praying, be specific!

I am aware that I do not need to specify when praying.

Only because *my God* knows what I am referring to.

I have never been amazed with myself...

I have always been the one who was negative and was so lost...

I am happy and content where I am in life now...

I am afraid, because what if I become the person who I once was?

Now I am aware of my thoughts and fears are out of my control

I probably should let God handle it.

I am happy!

I am blessed!

All my sad days are good ones...

I came into this residential shelter home willing to change...

The best part is I was able to bring my two blessings with me.

I am aware of God and all His greatness.

I am just so excited to be able to experience this opportunity

With the love of my life!

My twins!

In Jesus' Name, Amen.

March 2023

Heavenly Father,

Thank you for Your plan for us through Jesus your Son that we can have an abundant life through placing our faith in Him. Thank you, Jesus, for the gift of the Holy Spirit!

Thank you for the revival in our land in colleges, nine planned Jesus marches and further revival we do not even know about. In revival we pray Your love, humility, peace and discernment for Your people! We come praying repentant hearts for Your people.

Please Lord Jesus, forgive me for my pride, my insecurity, my tendency to control. I want to continually search my heart daily; that I will repent and lay everything at your feet, Jesus. Thank you for Your forgiveness and making The Way to do that.

Praying for revival in us, our city, fill us with Your love and boldness in the Gospel, to have more salt on our tongues.

We pray for the peace of Jerusalem and a hedge of protection around Israel, protection around our families and churches that are rightly dividing Your Word of Truth. Praise You! Thank You! In Jesus' Name, Amen.

Lord Jesus,

Thank you for making the way for me to come boldly into the throne room with my prayers.

My go-to prayer is "guard my heart and mind in Christ Jesus" from Philippians 4:7. Thank you!

I pray for my focus to stay on You, Jesus, an increased sensitivity to the Holy Spirit, a sharpened discernment, and to clothe myself in Your Whole Armor every morning.

Search my heart and reveal to me where I need to repent. Thank you for the promise of forgiveness.

In Jesus' Name, Amen

Seeing then that we have a High Priest who has passed through the heavens, Jesus the Son of God, let us hold fast to our confession. For we do not have a High Priest who cannot sympathize with our weaknesses, but was in all points tempted as we are, yet without sin. Let us therefore come boldly to the throne of grace, that we may obtain mercy and find grace to help in time of need.

—Ephesians 4:14-16

Part Three

Encouraging Words

Appreciation for First Responders
Mrs. Debby Williamson, Deputy Chief Reginald Winston,
Mrs. Bonnie Haak, Officer Thomas Anderson

***

Chapter 14

For the Children

Children. Grandchildren. All Children.

Integrity With Liberty: A Publication of At Liberty Bookstore

Editor Bonnie Haak:

> *We would do well to realize we are teaching our children something...by our choices and actions... by our words. Consistently teaching them every day. If we are people of integrity, our children will be of integrity. If we treat others with kindness and gentleness, likely our children will too. The kindest thing a father can do for his children is to love their mother. The kindest thing a mother can do for her children is to respect her husband. If we would like to make the greatest impact for the future, the way is through our children.*

***

My husband and I together have five remarkable grandchildren. Children are so amazing without even trying to be. Of course, our grandchildren have an unrivaled place in our hearts. Nothing else likens to our sons and their wives parenting their own children. Of course everyone knows, grandparenting is special because you spoil them and then give them back to Mom and Dad.

It's a little like freelancing.

***

As a young girl, somewhere I learned the joy of making ant farms. This was an activity I never tired of, and later I would teach my children and other willing children how to make an ant farm. The ant farm consisted of a gallon glass jar with a metal lid, enough dirt to fill the jar right to where it curves at the top, a soda pop lid, a small number of breadcrumbs and twenty-five-plus ants. Here are the instructions:

- Ask an adult to puncture the holes in the lid of your glass jar. Then fill your jar with dirt; shake it down, but don't pack it. Find a couple of sticks, about seven inches long. Look for an active ant colony hole. Hold the stick in the middle of the ant hole. Ants will climb on. Shake the ants off the stick over the opening of the gallon jar. Continue filling with ants.

- Take your ant farm inside. Add breadcrumbs and a capful of water. Place inside a dark closet for seven days.
- When you remove the gallon jar, you will have a full-fledged ant farm. You can watch the ants traveling through their tunnels. Kids love it. It is quite fun!

When I showed this to my nine-year-old son Ben, he took it to a whole new level. He graduated from the gallon jar to a wagon ant farm and would spend hours observing and taking care of his ants.

***

We grew some of the best tomatoes in town right in front of our home. Maybe it was the big eave on that side of the house. Maybe it was because I prayed when I planted. Or maybe it was the special mixture of peat moss and manure. Maybe it was the Miracle-Gro we were not too proud to use. We had six tomato plants, and they would produce enough tomatoes for a town block. Even the year when we had a storm where the golf-ball-size hail pummeled the tomato plants down to their stalks, they came back.

Our tomatoes were getting quite a reputation, so I started telling people we lived in the home that had the "dancing tomatoes" in front of the living room window; sometimes people came over to our home to see the dancing tomatoes. This reminded me of the beauty of having a little bit of an imagination.

***

I was given an opportunity to organize an Awana program and serve as the commander within our small town, where three local churches participated along with some children from the community.

Be diligent to present yourself approved to God, a worker who does not need to be ashamed, rightly dividing the word of truth.

—2 Timothy 2:15

Chapter 15
Building with the Basics
Simple. Ingenuous. Contented.

My brother Eddie is such a good example of simple faith. He said to me, "Bonnie, I am praying whether to go visit Mom this weekend" (he had a family of six). He was in Arizona, and Mom lived in Truth or Consequences, New Mexico. The next day Eddie called me and said, "Well, we are not going. I went to pick up the mail, and we got a really big electric bill."

Clearly, for me, it was a lesson in listening.

***

When our home was undergoing construction by my husband, our youngest son was observing his dad's every move. One day, I heard a noise coming from the backyard. I opened the door to find David successfully pulling siding off the house. He was three years old.

***

I was in the kitchen starting to prepare sausage, egg, and cheese sandwiches. Inside the egg carton were the last two eggs. My husband said to me, "It is OK. You and the boy can have the eggs; I will have sausage and cheese on my sandwich." He left the kitchen, and I continued preparing the sandwiches. When we sat down at the table, my husband noticed there was egg in his sandwich, and he asked me about it. I explained God had provided because when I opened the egg carton, lo and behold, there was the tallest egg I had ever seen. I cut that tall egg in half in the frying pan. Buying fresh eggs has added benefits!

***

When my husband, Bob, a skilled builder remodeled our home, it was a most interesting time for our family. We lived in it throughout the process, which took ten months.

I shared a picture of our living room and eating space (which was a card table) with a coworker; the ceiling was gone. The floor was still intact, but there came a time later when we were walking on floor joists. My coworker could not believe it, but the picture spoke a thousand words.

Throughout those ten months, we were without an argument. My two requests as Bob took us from 900 to 1800 square feet were for a large pantry in the kitchen and a bigger second bathroom. The pantry I think you can already understand; the second bathroom was because we only had one bathroom when I was pregnant with David, and there were five of us in the home. And then there were six. Women will certainly appreciate that request.

I left the building decisions to my husband, and I made the decisions for cooking and took care of our sons. At one point, when our kitchen was gutted, we had a dresser in the living room with our microwave on top for food preparations. The few real dishes we utilized I would place into a five-gallon bucket or two. There was no way I was willing to wash dishes in the bathtub, so I would take the bucket of dishes over to a friend's house, load them in her dishwasher, and engage in a good game of pinochle there at the kitchen table! A much-needed break.

When Bob reroofed our home, it was pretty interesting. He would get up at the crack of dawn and start to work before work. Our neighbor Ione Clontz, who was quite a character, would come out of her house and start yelling at Bob, *"You're crazy! Go back to bed!"*

***

My husband and I had an opportunity to host two boys and their pastor from Africa! I was nervous and called a sister-in-Christ, Wanda, to talk with her about it. She told me to take them to the grocery store after I picked them up at the church, (food is universally understood, right!)

Formed in 1984 as a ministry of Friends in the West, the African Children's choir – featuring children ages five to twelve – travel to raise funds for and awareness of the plight of children living in Sudan, Rwanda, Uganda, Kenya, Ghana and Nigeria.

I arrived at the church, greeted them and asked if they would like to go to the store. The twenty-five-year-old man gave me a big smile and two thumbs up. I was not sure they spoke English but found out that they did on our way to the store.

Inside the grocery store was an incredible experience for me as I watched the man teaching them as we pushed the grocery cart. *And the joy!* These were people who had lost one or both parents and endured hardships too horrific to imagine, and they were so *joy full*!

Once we got home, the two nine-year-old boys immediately took to our son, who appeared even taller with the boys, one on each side, holding onto David's arms.

We learned that there were to be no sugar and no TV for the next several days. This restriction is given to all host families. No sugar, in order to keep their teeth healthy, and their minds and bodies calm. No TV, in order to keep their minds and focus healthy. And I did notice that the twenty-for children in the choir had the brightest, whitest teeth. This was a real plus, because of their joy, they loved to smile!

The boys' eyes were as big as saucers when they saw our dog, Queenie, and I felt a little sheepish by the fact we had a dog bed in the living room.

Attending the performance of the African Children's choir was joyful and tearful at the same time for my husband and me. They were dressed colorfully, danced with rhythm, and sang from their hearts.

The youngest was six years old, the oldest twelve. The girls were bald, the same as the boys, as their culture does not allow girls to grow their hair until they reach sixteen years of age.

It was then, at the performance, that we realized Ivan, who was staying with us, was their pastor.

When Ivan and the boys were getting ready the next day to board the bus and sing at our local hospital, I asked Ivan, "Do we have time to pray?"

Ivan said, "We always have time to pray."

At mealtime, one of the boys would pray over the food. And I do mean *pray*. This precious prayer would usually last for a good five minutes. As I listened to that five minutes of a child's pure prayer was something that I could not have learned anywhere else.

Chapter 16

Traffic Lights

Yellow. Red. Green.

I liken action to traffic light colors works with a little bit of imagination.

In some ways, it can even be therapeutic.

Yellow signifies to slow down and ponder...

The color red, which signifies to stop...

- Flee liars.
- Flee faces stuck in the mirrors and cell phones.
- Flee reprobate minds.
- Flee child abuse and neglect.
- Flee bitter roots.
- Flee wily women.
- Flee all forms of witchcraft.

- Flee revenge.
- Flee perverts and molesters.
- Flee bullies.
- Flee abuse of drugs and alcohol.
- Flee arrogant pride.
- Flee jealousy.
- Flee sarcasm.
- Flee distraction.
- Flee deceit.
- Flee gushing flattery.
- Flee confusion.

Green signifies to go...

- Keep solid foundations.
- Keep good laws.
- Keep true measurements.
- Keep reading books.
- Keep modesty.
- Keep relationships real.
- Keep beautiful hair.
- Keep prayer.
- Keep edifying speech.
- Keep cooking good food.
- Keep good restaurants.
- Keep the children safe.
- Keep mentoring.

- Keep man caves.
- Keep discipline.
- Keep God's love.
- Keep the forgiveness of Jesus.
- Keep your Bible open.
- Keep parents and grandparents.
- Keep "Thank you," "You are welcome," "I am sorry," and "I forgive you."
- Keep good animals.
- Keep hospitality.
- Keep gentleness.
- Keep mercy.
- Keep respect.
- Keep integrity.
- Keep your word.

And don't forget to keep the light on for your loved One's return.

Chapter 17

Integrity with Liberty

Selected Excerpts from a Publication of At Liberty Bookstore

Does the content of what you participate in have integrity or not? Do you examine from time to time if you are exhibiting integrity? Once in a while, it is good to step back for a minute and examine what it is we are doing. We need to be people of integrity, we need to ask for integrity in our schools, in our community, in our homes. One thing for sure...there are certain places we can go to for guidance, a close friend walking in integrity, a mentor. The best one source is the Word of God. Then when we start to slip, and we will sometimes...we can go back to the Word that reminds us in a solid and constant way what it is we need to do to get back to where we need to be... people of integrity. When we have been sowing on good ground, it is but one step to get back to the Rock!

April 17, 2007

Integrity with Liberty is a publication that is written with liberty for a community that should benefit from receiving timely information in an honest, maybe not always popular, way. I have the highest respect for the liberty that we have in this country we live in, and I realize it came at a great cost. There are many liberties we have as citizens in this country, which can be exercised to benefit the community we reside in and to the nation as a whole. Because we are the nation. We are the people. We can make a difference if we are willing to step away from complacency and apathy.

It takes a little bit of time every day or so over the course of a longer time to make that difference. We cannot do everything, but we can do something. When we build a good foundation, it will be there when the time comes to go further.

Persistence is the key to a better way. Is there a better way? There is always a better way, not meaning to reinvent the wheel; in those areas that are struggling, oftentimes it takes just one person to be the spark to a small group of passionate, persistent people who will make the difference. A tremendous difference. If we get caught up in complaining and are unwilling to expend negative energy into a positive force for what we are concerned about begs a question. The question? Ask it of yourself, with liberty.

May 1, 2007

Sending packages overseas to our military has been a privilege for us for the last four years. I have said, "As long as I have the freedom to go to the store, then I will continue to try to send something to those serving overseas."

One important aspect of our packages is for us to acknowledge that without God this would not be possible. We were mindful to include a scripture verse, a prayer, a book...something that speaks about the Creator. This is lasting.

A package that our community sent over, upon receipt, the soldiers gathered around it, many were nervous about going on their first convoy. Opening the box, they acknowledged God's hand there.

Each soldier received their portion from the box, they prayed, and then they went out.

This report was given to me by Anna, the mother of one of those soldiers.

And so...we are reminded again.

May 8, 2007

Our Father in Heaven,

I pray that we will be mindful of the liberty and freedom we have in this country and remember where it has come from. I pray that our nation will follow Your precepts established at the founding of this country.

I pray for the men and women who are serving. I pray for Your protection over them, that they will know Your Presence, leading and guiding as they serve. I pray for their families for Your strength in times of uncertainty.

I pray for those who have lost loved ones, for comfort and an understanding that You will carry them through.

In the name of Jesus,

Amen.

May 8, 2007

As the Lord continues to bless the unity of His Church, some of God's people received a blessing as the Spirit did freshly fall upon those saints in last Sunday's morning worship service, where two church families were together in attendance.

Guest speaker Minister Green brought forth the Word of God, reminding the people in the waiting congregation that we are saved, sanctified, and filled with the Holy Ghost. *He spoke that God is looking for the true worshippers, stating we all have a Samaria, and we are to go there by the Power of the Holy Spirit and stand firm in those places that God puts us in.*

Minister Green preached from the book of John, chapter four, about Jesus's encounter with the woman at the well. He brought forth Acts 1:8, and also 8:5–13.

Minister Green shared his testimony of how he came to know the Lord personally in 1989, and he has been serving Him ever since.

Two soldiers in our midst confirmed the well of water that was provided by prayer on a well-traveled road for the soldiers in Iraq, because they were there.

A Christian brother in blessing the Communion cup, asked for God's forgiveness of things he had previously held in his heart against his Christian brother of a different race. This confession brought with it tears of healing and forgiveness into the sanctuary. True humility will always bring in the Holy Spirit's Presence.

We were in that waiting congregation. Minister Green had been invited to bring the Word and his church family by our pastor in his absence.

***

At a later time, my husband and I were at a community event when folks started going forward to the front where local pastors stood and an invitation had been made. Minister Green called me in his authoritative voice, "Sister Haak, get up here and pray for these people." And I did, without hesitation or reservation!

On one occasion when I attended Elder Green's home church, he was preaching, and said, "I am a soldier in the military, but I am a soldier for Jesus first!" He had the biggest heart for Jesus I had ever witnessed.

Stop. Pray. Discern. SELAH.

Chapter 18

Moving *Forward*

Get Ready. Get Set. Go!

Maya: Her best day was the moment she said "yes" to Jesus. It did not look how she expected, but she knew it was Him. He sent her to Texas into a jail cell. She sat in the jail cell for ninety days, all of which she lay in a bed reading the KJV Bible for at least twelve to thirteen hours a day, every day.

Then the Holy Spirit came upon her, and she thought it was a neurological problem she was feeling, until an older woman walked by, talking to another lady, and saying, "My gran-mama said when you feel electricity in your body, that is the Holy Spirit."

Maya said to herself, "Holy Spirit?" She looked in the back of the Bible, and it directed her to the book of John. And then it hit her, and she said, "*This is You?*" And there came the familiar jolt of electricity confirming to her: Yes!

Truthfully, Maya has never been the same since that day in 2008. It is difficult to place into mere words the freedom and victory He has given her in life and the gratitude she has toward Him.

If she could have fast-forwarded the next sixteen years, she would have never been able to imagine the life He has given her to this day, which looks like a life overhaul.

Today Maya understands her first-place ministry, the home life ministry for her children who came to her at the age of forty years old, and a husband who is truly an example of a godly man of valor and strength. All because of God.

Recently Maya has been blessed to live in a residential shelter home for a "season" to rest and gain ground on this ministry she calls motherhood.

She believes this to be the one scripture that sums up her life moving forward is a special gift from God for her encouragement.

For you were bought at a price; therefore, glorify God in your body and in your spirit, which are God's.

—1 Corinthians 6:20

So Maya lives her life for Christ and has become a living testimony of the handiwork of His living Spirit who resides in her.

Praise Jesus!

***

Together, my husband and I made the decision to screen-fast, which led to an astonishing result! Technology has advanced by leaps and bounds in the past couple of decades. There is much to be said regarding the benefit of technology. On the other hand, there are compelling concerns regarding the grip technology holds for all ages in our society today.

The key was a commitment to fast from all screens, except for work purposes, one day a week and one hour daily.

This screen-fast included our cell phones, other than phone calls or activities for work purposes. What we found inside this screen-fast commitment was the obvious: more time to read, more focused conversations, card games or sport games with the family, motorcycle rides, loving (ooh-la-la), more incentive to take care of necessary chores, and of course more time to cook.

My dependence on screens, with the cell phone and TV, was stealing my time and thoughts became clear to me that my brain was not functioning the way it used to regarding creativity, assessing, resting, evaluating, planning, relationship keeping...the list goes on. Science has proven that sleep heals the body and brain. What benefit does screen-fasting then bring to the brain?

The most exciting result I gained from the screen-fast was a renewed awareness to put into action those things that truly mattered to me…all because of gaining a sharper sense of clarity and the availability of more time!

Screen-fasting held this result for me: I felt years younger and confident to act now rather than later! Funnily, it was like going back to where I was before this advancement of digital technology. It affected my mind by kicking it into an evaluation mode on the here and now. I started choosing each new morning with deliberation, which led to exhilaration, resulting in freedom.

The result?

A purposed freedom to decide where I wanted to go and how to get there, coupled with clarity and an increase in time leading the way!

Can you imagine the possibilities in this same space?

Chapter 19

Readers' Reflection

You Haven't Come This Far to Just Come This Far

Listening for your best first day?

Do not hurry it; once you have it, do not second-guess it!

Once you have your first best day, listen to your heart for more best days!

Look for applications of these best days for today and beyond!

Share with your loved ones your memories again!

Write about your first best day. Think of your best days and write about the first one that comes to your mind.

Oh, and the "same" thing we all have in common is...we were all children once!

More Best Days

Write some memories of your best days. As these best days come to life again inside your memory and heart, share with your family and friends.

Navigating Traffic Lights

Yellow. Red. Green.

<mark>Yellow signifies to slow down and ponder...</mark>

Starting with the color red, which signifies to stop...

Finally, the best is yet to come—Green signifies to go...

Screen-Fasting Commitment

Hour screen-fasting, every day, same hour: Consider dinner time for meal prep and dining. This one is rich.

And/or

Hour segments screen-fasting. Pick a block of hours for fasting same day of the week.

And/or

Twenty-four-hour screen-fasting (other than work). Phone calls are OK because they do not require the screen. Consider keeping the same day of the week, every week.

If you find yourself willing, but not ready, remember to give yourself some grace.

We cannot do everything, but we can do something.

Thank you, reader, for taking the time to consider this book in the busyness of life!

Thank you to those individuals who took the time to share their first best day. So amazing are they!

Special thanks to Maya for her labor of love and gifting for the illustrations of the Bridge!

Email Bonnie: yourbestdays.2024@gmail.com
Connect with Bonnie: https://www.linkedin.com

Online Resources

The Grace Alliance (www.mentalhealthgracealliance.org)
Blue Letter Bible (www.blueletterbible.org)
National Alliance on Mental Illness (www.nami.org)
National Institute of Mental Health (www.nimh.nih.gov)
WebMD (www.webmd.com)
MedicineNet Healthcare (www.medicinenet.com)

Dial 988 for the Suicide and Crisis Lifeline.
When people call, text, or chat with the 988 Lifeline, they are connected to trained crisis counselors who are part of the existing 988 Lifeline network, made up of over 200 local crisis centers. These crisis counselors are trained to provide free and confidential emotional support and crisis counseling to people in suicidal crisis or emotional distress and connect them to resources. These services are available twenty-four hours a day, seven days a week, across the United States.

For more information, visit www.988lifeline.org.

Awana is a global nonprofit organization fueled by the generous support of individuals, churches, and organizations to accomplish our mission of equipping leaders to reach kids with the gospel and engage them in lifelong discipleship. Contributions to Awana are tax-deductible as allowed by law. Awana has complete discretion and control over the use of donated funds.

The Awana organization was established in 1950 in the United States, founded by Lance Latham.

With an unwavering commitment to the gospel, Awana is being used to reach more than six million kids every week in 135 countries, giving children and youth from every background an opportunity to know, love, and serve Jesus for a lifetime. Find out how Awana can serve you in reaching kids in both your local community and around the world for Jesus, for life.

Visit www.awana.org for more information.

A Psalm. A Song at the dedication of the house of David. I will extol You, O LORD, for You have lifted me up, And have not let my foes rejoice over me. O LORD my God, I cried out to You, And You healed me. O LORD, You brought my soul up from the grave; You have kept me alive, that I should not go down to the pit. Sing praise to the LORD, you saints of His, And give thanks at the remembrance of His holy name. For His anger (is but for) a moment, His favor (is for) life; Weeping may endure for a night, But joy (comes) in the morning.

—Psalm 30:1–5

Acknowledgements

With special thanks to my Publishing Agent, Julia Phelps, an encourager, and a real breath of fresh air; Publishing Editor Jordan, one of the finest experiences of my life; and Project Manager Weston Richards, a partnership of intense and exhilarating work.

To my husband the love of my life, Bob, of thirty-nine years, through the valleys and on the mountain tops; we were called to be a team, with Jesus at the head of our marriage.

My precious family, and also now their families, who have given me countless memories for the best days of my life; my adventurous birth family and loving extended family, who by their nature inspired writings in this book; and my church family, the place where iron sharpens iron, who have challenged, and loved me along this glorious journey we are on together.

Mrs. Debby Williamson, in this book development, by her character stepped into the "shoes of encouragement," my mom wore for me, big shoes.

Ana McNabb, psychiatric nurse practitioner, compassionately and humbly serving in the mental health field.

Brandi Marie, who loved me enough to have the courage to ask an important question during an intense time of trials in my life.

Sarah Wilinski, who took the time in her busy schedule to review the draft, and opened her heart, encouragement, and some doors for me.

Mary McGhee, for poring over the draft, who is solid in friendship and Christianity.

Jason Castano, mi Hermano en Cristo, whose godly counsel is always on-point.

All pastors and teachers who rightly divide the Word of truth.

And Jesus Christ for sacrificially giving His life, for me to believe, and sending the leading of the Holy Spirit who forever speaks to my heart.

Bonnie Haak, a native Arizonan, currently lives on the corner of peace and quiet within a small city in Arizona. She and her husband of thirty-nine years have a blended family of four sons, three daughters-in-law, and five grandchildren. She loves hugs, talking with her family and grandchildren, and praying for people on the spot. She enjoys cooking good food, reading in bed when it is raining, collecting interesting rocks, planting a garden, and watching her dogs Laverne and Shirley romp in the living room. Bonnie's love of writing has been lifelong and she is grateful to be partnering with Palmetto Publishing for such a time as this.